Odes and Prose for Older Women

– DIANA WELLS –
with illustrations by Sandy Cluff

An environmentally friendly book printed and bound in England by
www.printondemand-worldwide.com

Mixed Sources
Product group from well-managed
forests, and other controlled sources
www.fsc.org Cert no. TT-COC-002641
© 1996 Forest Stewardship Council
FSC

PEFC
PEFC/16-33-415

PEFC Certified
This product is
from sustainably
managed forests
and controlled
sources
www.pefc.org

This book is made entirely of chain-of-custody materials

www.fast-print.net/store.php

ODES AND PROSE FOR OLDER WOMEN
Copyright © Diana Wells 2013

The right of Diana Wells to be identified as the author of this work has
been asserted by her in accordance with the Copyright, Designs and
Patents Act 1988 and any subsequent amendments thereto.

A catalogue record for this book is available from the British Library

ISBN 978-178035-683-9

First published 2013 by
FASTPRINT PUBLISHING
Peterborough, England.

This book is dedicated to my husband, William, with love and thanks. Also for my beloved children, Charlotte, Robert and Simon – they are my greatest achievement.

Index

Fantasy Of Success

In my latest reverie
Maggie Smith said to me
'I do hope I can recite your verse
Or has Judi Dench got there first'?

Old And Alone

I'm 76 and on my own
My husband has died and my children have flown
The nest as well they should
And their children don't respect me as I feel they could.

So I'm bored with the effort of being content
Of rounding my Autumn of a life well spent
With shopping and bridge games and insincere smiles
I want sex and excitement – use my feminine wiles
While I've got them – I'm not blind
To the sagging, the age spots and lined
I may be, but my soul and my humour are still 23.

As I lift my skin up round my eyes every day
Rub in creams, apply make-up, comb my hair and then
   spray
I reflect on my future – Will someone appear?
P'raps today I will meet him – to call him 'my dear'

Well the days, weeks and months pass and I hasten to add
That I've tried every avenue, some good – mostly bad.
My misunderstood motives caused gossip and stress
In my circle of ladies – now they couldn't care less

About me – they say I have changed and their friendship
    abused
Feeling sad and rejected, defeated and old, I've got one
    more idea – I'll go on a cruise.

I've got plenty of money – no more need to invest
Except in designer stuff – I must look my best
For the West Indies trip in a small six star vessel
Leaving Tower Bridge next week and just so there's no
    hassle
And everyone knows that I'm not poor, lost or meek
I've decided to stay in the Capricorn Suite.

On boarding the craft from my hired limousine
I was wafted past others more lowly than me
Imperiously accepting their grovelling attention
And secretly hoping that EVERYONE had seen
The splendid arrival of this important Queen Bee.
'Have a glass of champagne; the maid will do that; where
    would you like dinner?
I know the Captain is free'
Anything I asked for, anything I wanted –
The smallest whim or great desire – everything was
    granted.

I settled in quickly to my role of largesse
Invitations – cocktails, dinner – a reason to dress
In all that designer-wear, silk and cashmere galore
Discarding my rejects in a pile on the floor
For the maid to hang up – it's her role in life
And I never then considered she might be mother and
    wife
That she might feel lost, upset and alone
Providing for her family in their Philippino home.

Still, on with my task of finding a man
He could look like Sean Connery or Piers Brosnan
But on that first evening, nowhere could I see
The tall handsome man with the lost lonely smile,
    scanning the rooms
and looking for …. me.

That second evening, on our Westerly way
Tired and discouraged from filling my day
With meaningless chatter, poor games and a lecture
I sat down in the lounge for a drink with a stranger
We had just raised our glasses, pinkies up, in a toast
When I suddenly saw him, my man, softly smiling
 With a badge saying 'Gentleman Host'.

'Can I join you Ladies?' the voice deep and mellow
was just the right timbre. I felt good in my yellow
A new dress, which I felt, showed my figure and cleavage
and I managed to stand up without using leverage.
'How kind' I was gracious, shook his hand saw his name
'How do you do Ken. Nice to meet you – I'm Elaine'

I couldn't halt my lip curling with distaste
As with inappropriate and rather 'common' haste
the other woman murmured and rose to her feet
She was younger than I was, well turned-out and petite
With languid gesture I did my best
To show sophisticated breeding. My first real test!

We sat with five others for Dinner – a very long-winded
    affair
I waved away several waiters, who were scurrying
    everywhere

distracting my concentrated efforts at seducing the man
    on my right
I was certain he found me alluring. I began hoping he
    might spend the night
I had champagne on ice; a silk nightie brand new. I'd
    wear nothing at all underneath.
But that other woman smiled shyly and slyly, gaily
    showing her pearly white teeth.

Stress levels rose beyond reason and I started to babble
    and witter
To the obvious amusement of others and there started a
    general titter.
'Would you like to come to the Night Club? It would be
    lovely to dance
with a lady as gorgeous as you.' He said to her. I clearly
    had no chance.
'Oh, I'd love to' cooed the other, and gave me a
    triumphant smile
I wanted to smack her quite badly, she was like a
    victorious child.

The following days passed by slowly and I relished my
    calm isolation
As I hid in the theatre or stateroom. I refused to accept
    invitations.
And even those outings ashore, booked and paid for and
    tickets received
Were no use to me now as I fretted and paced, smoked
    and drank and grieved.
'Poor me' I wailed to the roaring sea as I stood in the cold
    on my balcony
This was worse than the life I was used to at home, and I
    never had felt this lonely.

As we sailed into England, through Southampton Sound,
    I felt the tears in my eyes
Because no-one on board would miss me and whilst they
    were saying 'goodbyes'
Swopping numbers, addresses, making dates to meet
    again
There was not one other person that I could call 'friend'.
And the last bloody straw was when Ken and 'The Cow'
    walked hand-in-hand to the quay
She turned, smiling gaily and waved like a queen, her
    eyes were fixed on me.

Back home in my flat, which felt cold, musty and dank
I turned on the heating, poured a large gin and sank
Deep into my sofa, feeling worse than before
I lifted the mail that had lain on the floor
The usual junk, but, hello what's this - a blue embossed
    envelope with fountain pen ink.
'Dear Elaine' it said 'remember me? We last met when
    we were 23.
I'm a widower now, hate being alone. I would love to see
    you. What do you think?'

HOORAY!

Edie

I can remember when 'Edie was a Lady'
Before her body thickened and her dealings became
    shady.
When her perm was tight and mascara robust
When she still thought she could satisfy her lust.

Edie never married – she never found one good enough.
She said she'd had her offers but they were 'common,
    rude and rough'.
So she'd waited, watched and prayed for the perfect type
    of lad
Until just past her forties when her eyes fell on my Dad!

She was working as our cleaner but her aspirations vast
Included wearing décolletage, high heels and, from her
    past
There seemed a huge array of tiny skirts and lacy tops
Which she wore with glee and giggles as she danced
    around her mop.

My Father couldn't cope of course and though he tried to
    smile
You could tell from body language that he'd rather be a
    mile
At least away from Edie's obvious fervour
Eventually he asked for help from his best friend, my
    mother.

My Mother laughed uproariously but realised her duty
Taking charge of the situation following Dad's fraught
    entreaty.
She had, in truth, noticed that the housework had grown
    sloppy
With a hard to eradicate constant whiff of 'California
    Poppy'.

Edie still tried everything from allowing her top to dip
To wearing just her petticoat, a purple and coffee lace slip
Which she claimed was necessary on this 'oh so hot day'
Before staging a faint with fragile moan as poor Dad
    passed her way.

But Edie hadn't reckoned on my mother being there
And took the news of her sacking with cold incredulous
    stare.
'He loves me, I know it' she pawed at my father who
    pushed her away.
We settled down but life at home was pretty boring after
    that day.

Martha And Philip

In the afternoon she watched him as he slept. She noted the rhythm of his breathing with occasional gentle wet pumps of a snore. She looked at his feet – good feet for a man in his sixties - no sign of corns or cracked skin - just a small skein of veins networking underneath each ankle. 'His hair is really thinning now' she thought as he pulled one arm down from the top of his head and moved the thicker mass away from an expanding baldness further back. 'He's still nice looking' she realised and smiled. 'I love him' she thought.

They had come a long way, Philip and Martha. The difficult days, the almost catastrophic rows were over. She had allowed, as the years passed, a feeling of calm serenity to take over. She'd believed, eventually, that the sense of endless chaos to which she had become inured, were over. She was no longer permanently watchful, listening, scenting the next blow to herald another dangerous situation.

Going on a cruise had been Philip's idea. 'I'm not a natural cruiser' she had laughed at him when he'd first raised it. His deep scowl instantly wiped the smile from Martha's face. Capitulation was easy; easier than watching the face that she loved deepen into a concrete mask smeared by deepening cracks of displeasure. She always gave in and he was used to it now. She thought she knew the rules and never expected a return to the old days when she lived on a knife-edge between her heightened sensitivity and his brutal thoughtlessness.

They were on a large table for dinner that evening. She glanced across regularly to check if all was well or if he needed rescuing from one of the women at his side. Not a tolerant man, but he'd never let it show to strangers, and she was always there to help.

Martha took an interest in other older couples – there were plenty of them on the ship, and they seemed to her to be demonstrably happy. 'Not like us – not really' she'd thought. Sadly she glanced quickly across the table. Philip pulled a face at her, indicating, with flickering lashes, that neither woman at his side was pleasing him.

'Your husband's career has been quite extraordinary' the American on Martha's left – a doctor from New York, was engaging her in conversation. They had already discussed his job and his decision not to retire; his wife of five years sitting the far end of the table to whom he had blown a kiss when they were seated. They had talked about the weather, the children and the destinations on the cruise and then each had turned to their other companion on the other side to follow the format of good manners at a formal dinner table. Now, the doctor had turned to her again.

Martha started to gabble 'Oh, my life was completely chaotic until I met Philip'. They both looked across the table and Philip said 'what?' in that testy way Martha dreaded. 'No, nothing' she called gaily, certainly not wishing to repeat what she had just said in a louder voice for everyone to hear. But, Philip's scowl deepened as he looked meaningfully at Martha's glass of wine (her second of the evening) and he started muttering and shaking his head. Feeling the thrill of dread, Martha fought to understand – was Philip trying to convey that she drank too much and that this was a problem for him? Martha stopped breathing, mesmerised by her husband's face and his betrayal, not to mention the injustice of his indication that she was a drinker. He knew, of course, that both her parents were heavy drinkers and he knew that her first husband was an alcoholic. In that seemingly endless moment, feeling the blood drain from her face and her trust in her husband eradicated, the loss of security and the loneliness she thought had gone forever, returned.

'Some people don't take compliments well' said the voice at her side. Turning slowly to face him, Claire fought for her composure but she could see that she'd failed and that this stranger knew how desolate she felt. He put his hand on her arm in a gesture of sympathy.

'Please don't' she said and deliberately picked up her glass to drink, before thanking the waiter for a refill.

My Cat Said

My cat said:
"Why are you moving that pencil unless it's to share and
 play?"
She jumped and grabbed with teeth and claws newly
 sharpened that day.
My eyebrows were just about finished so I reached for a
 tube I prefer
"Mine" she screeched happily pouncing, knocking my
 lipstick away

My cat said:
"Sorree" she sat down beside me, turned round and
 levered her way
to the smallest part of my stool obliging me to shift away
dropping cosmetics all over the floor – I was getting very
 fed up
"Go away" I pushed at my kitten, wishing I'd bought a
 pup.

My cat said:
"Don't say you are off out again – not so soon.
I've been waiting around for hours
For something to do, with one of you two.
I'm tired of breaking the flowers"

My cat said:
'There's my funny old man coming in through the door
I expect he'll throw himself down prone on the floor
I'll wander over for a rub and a chat
But I'm getting worried he thinks HE is the cat.

My cat said:
"Why did you leave me in the horrible cattery,
Where we're lined up like chickens in that sort of battery.
Just wait till we get home and I'll make you pay
I'm not going to forgive you, whatever you say".

My cat said:
'I'm really very happy when you give me my food
and whilst what you give me is often quite good
might I have some salmon or a little bit of chick
or your fillet steak – could I have a lick?

My cat said:
'Well, it's been nice seeing you - Now I must go out
since my friends are all waiting for my morning shout.
I'll kill a few things, perhaps a bird, surely a mouse
And I'll be back later when you've cleaned the house'.

The Graduation

July is the time when students endure
Graduation day with all its' allure
The parents at last are allowed to come in
To this seat of learning and this den of sin.

The professors and tutors polite but bored
Force some conversation with this lowly hoard
Of mothers and fathers and siblings alike
Who come as a contrast to their clever tike.

The family convinced that their child is so brilliant
But the truth is it's easy if you're quite resilient
To heaps of booze, cheap food and the rest
Much sleeping and chatting with occasional tests.

Ensconced in the Sports Hall, we hope to begin
We've endured the formal music, a really nasty din
Of both organ and brass, a horrid, sorry combination
We care not, we're here for our own young sensation

He's sitting in the back with all his friends and peers
The camera pans across them and there are shouts and
    jeers
As excitedly they share this time before each nervous one

is called to accept the paper, which records what they
have done.

The procession enters slowly and they look rather a hoot
Sitting in the front row I resist putting out my foot
Their po-faces do not falter, they maintain the stoic mask
Of intellectual excellence which compels them to this
task.

The group has now been seated atop the flowered dais
One rises from the front and we wait for what he says
About our little darlings and the university
Which is, of course, the best there is, especially his
faculty.

The names are called and as they pass the vice-chancellor
expects
Each one of them to acknowledge him but some just
bend their necks
Whilst mine, the perfect boy, does well and bows with
some panache
Before this man who smiles before he strokes his little
'tache.

What next, oh yes, the photographs to record this special
day
I know better than to fuss and let the expert have her way
Of tidying up my handsome son, arranging his gown and
tassle
Before moving behind her camera and saving me the
hassle.

We are offered more drinks in 'hospitality'
And a chance to meet more of his friends and their
family

My beloved son has made a few, lots of girls I see
But the days are over now when he will come home to
    me.

I'm very proud. It's all as we planned it
He's well on his way and he's set a high standard
Maybe one day he'll sit at the front on a chair
On a dais just like that one. A bright future is clear.

Miss Gladys Campion – Aged 91

Have you been to visit the old in a home
They're cared for but usually feel so alone
Even though they're together in a lounge nice and bright
They're propped up in the chairs, rigid, upright.

Of course when you're old you don't need so much sleep
And the effort of daily life forces you deep
Into reserves of stamina, patience and courage
When your battery for energy has failed to manage.

I met one such person – a lady called Gladys
Who wears lace at her throat and a face full of sadness
Her skin is like paper, her hair thin and grey
But her eyes hold your attention and she has much to
say.

She has been in the home for nigh on 16 years
When her own mother died and her world full of fears
Became too much to process, too much to endure
And hell was her loneliness, hopelessness pure.

So at 91, she sits there unable to see
Gently waiting for company and a nice cup of tea

And a chance to relive the days of her youth
T'was a time with no reason to keep her aloof.

She told me that others there think she is crazy
When remembering before being forced to be lazy
She says she told Churchill the nation should pray
And smiles confident it was she paved the way.

Her great love was Harold – a local born lad
Killed defending the capital – she nearly went mad
She talks of her school friends when nine of them died
In front of her – strafed in a ditch. Well, I nearly cried.

I saw a photo when aged 24
Gladys sits at her war desk looking busy, assured
Her knitting is waiting in case there's a quiet spell
To help wartime effort. She made blankets as well.

We all ought to listen to old ones like Gladys
Mostly the old are not stupid, and one big sadness
Is that all of those episodes, stories and histories
Are lost in the ether when they have left us.

Ferneic Spache

ŭ = absent sound

'Owver ere' Fred shouted to his son from the other side of the Salon. 'Woŭ do yer fink yer doin? Yer should be graftin.'

Daryl went to his father. 'Weŭ' replied the shining child 'Oim finkin abart goin to universiŭy. Innit'. He put his hand on the older man's shoulder. 'Av you noŭist tha oil them big chaises on t'telly spake proper and know loads of stuff? Weŭ, Oi…. Fink…Oi wan to end up a big chaise.'

'Oh shuŭ up will yer' said Fred. 'Ooze gonna pie for iŭ do yer fink? Cos iŭ snot in moi power to pie for toim-wasting fings loik thaŭ.

'Ow can iŭ be toim-wastin Dad? Would you ravver Oi wenin fer air-care loik you?

'Wewll, Oi woz hopin' thaŭ in toime you moight wanna tike over the bizniz. Yeah'.

'Oh shu-up will ya. Oive goŭ bigger plansanaŭ buŭ fanks anywhy.' Daryl swept the cut hair away from under the chair where his father had been working.

The voice that went with the perm behind it turned to Daryl 'Young man' she croaked, 'It's offally good to hear of your ambition. Maybe one day you'll be able to live in a nice hise like I do. It's frateful that your father won't support you. What would you like to be eventually?'

Daryl looked at the woman, noting the bulbous purple nose, the leaking lined eyes and the caked foundation around her mouth and chin. 'A future client?' he wondered.

He grinned at the woman. 'Oi reelly am keen to be a pafologist, like on the telly. I can cuŭ up all sorts of fings then calnI?

'Oim genome na Dad. Seeya'.

Sleeping With Ashes

If you squeeze your eyes almost until they are shut but you can see your lashes this will give you the best idea of how it might feel to be half-awake and half-asleep. This was how I spent two whole nights.

On the second night I had delayed going to bed until some hours later than usual, hoping that I would forget what was downstairs and drift into a seamless, dreamless sleep. Some hope.

'Get into the foetal position' I told myself repeatedly as I tossed and turned, trying to find the perfect rest. But my eyes kept drifting open towards the little computer-activated glow, lights that meant the television, printer and myriad other gadgets were on 'standby', in the next room. Eventually nature took over and I lolled into a restless state of slumber.

This was my son's house and I stayed there alone whilst he was in hospital. He wasn't critical but he was miserable and, since his father's death three months earlier, events seemed to have piled on top of him. I was there to visit him daily, take him what he needed, clean his house, do his ironing etc. Generally to give this young man, my child, the support he needed.

It's a sweet house. I really like it. The bedroom and sitting room are upstairs and the kitchen, bathroom and an assortment of huge and threatening fitness machinery is downstairs. The conversion from barn has been well done and the under-floor heating works well under the traditional flagstones.

There as another addition, but very unwelcome as far as I was concerned – it's a thick manila carrier bag, sitting on the floor nestled in between a pile of pictures and a Neanderthal looking machine. Inside there was a strong deep purple cardboard box with a label on the top advertising the contents as my first husband's ashes, along with the date of cremation some weeks previously.

When I first heard the noise, I assumed it was a pipe clicking, or a floorboard creaking in the quiet of deep night. As the volume increased slightly, my attention was caught. I didn't feel afraid so much as accepting of the inevitable.

I watched calmly as a shadow approached. Not quite a human form, more of a blurred cloud, perpendicular and swirling. I knew who it was from the walk – cocky and arrogant. I started to say the Lord's prayer in my head.

The image stopped at the end of the bed and I felt the scrutiny of something that I couldn't really see but which I recognised – Oh, I knew quite well whose image this was. It wasn't just surveillance either – there was a definite element of threat and I assumed, without resistance, that this was the retribution I should have expected from the husband that I had left and abandoned to his fate. My stillness was matched – there wasn't the faintest sound, not even from the humming refrigerator downstairs or the wind swirling above the skylights.

There was no communication apart from the image and atmosphere. I didn't know if some ghostly and unwelcome voice would suddenly start up? If so, what would he say?

Would I have had any sort of response should this scene develop? I had no idea but merely waited, feeling again the sorrow of wasted years with the father of my children, the drunken rows and the sexual demands from someone whose appeal had long gone. Replenished anguish of awareness of his suffering in the long years since we parted and my knowledge of this desperation and loneliness caused me to expect violence that did not come. Instead, we remained in this state of limbo whilst I remembered.

Starting with the happy times – and we were happy – I could not have foreseen his dependence on alcohol, until that first evening when I suddenly knew with a shock like a fist into the stomach, that we were in trouble. The baby, our beautiful daughter, was three months old and he came home from work night after night, almost unable to stand but finding the way to the drinks in the kitchen cupboard. There were so many evenings like this and then one day I'd had enough and told him I'd leave him if things didn't change. Where exactly I thought I was going to go with a tiny baby, no parents, no money and no job, I can't remember. He stopped for a while and then the whole cycle would begin again and each time I asked him what was the matter for him to have to become inebriated all the time when he had a beautiful wife and child? He always looked sad and promised and promised and promised.

He provided well and took pride in this – but to me it was only money and whilst I wanted to 'pay the piper', I did not want more – just a simple life.

People think it's easy to leave a marriage. It isn't. So the years passed and we had two sons. Three wonderful children – the joy of my life, and they became my focus my entire raison d'etre.

I think he had affairs. I didn't care, in fact in a little recess, tucked well away from view, I hoped that he might come home one day and say that he had met someone else. Now wouldn't that have been tidy?

Later there came a deep throbbing and rumbling as if an approach from a very great distance. The presence at the end of the bed seemed confused and angered by an interruption in its own visit.

I waited, breathless with shock and fright but, as the rushing and crashing became louder and, therefore, closer, I found that I was interested too. Who was this? Which of the many that had gone before me was coming to communicate?

Lights flashed psychedelically and more vividly even, as the frame grew larger.

It was Oliver. As he approached, I knew that I was grinning broadly and held out one arm in greeting.

'You wouldn't be able to feel my touch. So I won't bother'. He laughed - always amiable and entertaining.

The two images turned towards each other. The first arrival gave a tentative nod and lifted to one side as if to shake hands.

'Don't bother with any of that nonsense Guy' Oliver snarled. 'You must now realise that I observed everything that was happening to my little sister here?'

Guy's hand went down but the shoulders rose aggressively.

'Oh for Goodness sake' snapped Oliver. 'I know that you haven't been with us long but surely even you must have worked out that there is no place for your sort of human behaviour? Actually before too long you will realise that there is no enmity, no anger. In fact Guy I'm really annoyed that you have provoked that response from me anyway.'

Guy's image slumps.

I could feel my heart thumping so I knew that I was not dead as well, but my main sensation was as if I had been heavily drugged and couldn't properly open my eyes, lift my head from the pillow or speak.

The sun shone brightly through the roof-light and warmed the room. I reached for my bag and removed the small leather book that I carry everywhere. I glanced at the photographs of those that I love and find Oliver's. Taken the summer he died, he is sitting on the cliff-top, his back to the sea, the wind in his hair and that wonderful smile in place. I ran my finger over his face, remembering. 'Thank you big brother' I said and give him a kiss.

Fantasy – Sedan Chair

Imagine yourself on a golf course sublime
Where the days are quite perfect and the sun always
    shines
Where each shot that you take ends up as the kind
That you wanted, and hoped for, and had fixed in your
    mind.

In my fantasy there's no labour, no club heads to wipe
Everything's done by the young men, the sort that I like
With lovely tight buttocks, oiled skin and fair hair
Who bear me along in my big sedan chair.

I lie back on my cushions, serene and content
As my personal sports psycho explains that I bent
My left knee too soon and my hip moved again
Whilst I dip into the crystal which holds my champagne.

But really each shot I perform is a success
I'm ten under par now, not worried or stressed
A little green grape is about to be eaten
And I check on the state of my friend being beaten.

It's Marion of course and she's puce in the face
Vexed beyond reason, her language a disgrace
She's thumping the ground after another bad shot

Having tried everything, including Luther's swing pot.

She glares at me now and started to say
That she would report me to the ELGA
'Oh stop all your nonsense' I laughingly beckon
Come up here with me. Now what do you reckon?'

She loves it of course, bobbing along on my chair
And when the ground staff stop raking the bunkers to
    stare
She waves at them languidly 'Hello my good man.
We need more Champagne here. Come on quick as you
    can.'

So, giggling uproariously we finish our game
I'm delighted to tell her the score's still the same
That I'm only five up on her but it could have been more
We're both certainly good enough to join in the tour.

Fish Swimming In Water
IN THE STYLE OF E.E. CUMMINGS

We-ed to

      Lil-Y al(gae

GRUB?

Drag-on (fly?)
      Over

(w-a)s raindrops

Smo0othly-fin-under

Hopeful(ness)ly

(rO-ck)

hom

E

Deeply.

d.c.wells

Mr. Malapropism P

He often says 'profiterole' when I know he means
    peripheral
And I'm sure he thinks that 'profligate' is something
    quite acceptable.
To prognosticate he will assert is to do with diagnosis
And progesterone has been confused with a form of
    halitosis.

To proliferate to him means holding forth and being a
    bore
There's another word for massive reproduction he'll be
    sure.
The profundity of his wisdom must date back to a
    progenitor
Procrastination of traditional learning a matter of
    conjecture.

Prevarication of any sort just gets up his proboscis
He will assert the medical name for nose is still
    prosthesis.
Prescience is understood as an alarming lack of patience.
He loves to eat peripherals, with chocolate on for
    preference.

Although he is a pragmatist, a pirate and a predator
With a preponderance of stories – he's sure he's a realtor.
His main preoccupation now without being too
    pretentious
Is to preserve his principals without seeming too
    preposterous

His primeval instincts have succumbed; I have him on
    probation
Now the prolongation of his life is his main
    preoccupation
His prostrate gland from years of use was giving him
    some worry
The medic was told in certain tones 'I'm not giving that
    up in a hurry'.

So this professor of malapropism over words beginning
    with P
Will gladly talk about those happy times when he was at
    sea
He holds a clear prospective about what his future holds
And I wait with interest, watching him, to see how things
    unfold.

My Sister's Boyfriend

My name is Mary, my sister is Sue
She was wringing her hands, saying 'What should I do?'
A young man was hounding her - his name was Hugh
But she couldn't bear him and he had no clue.

Sue said 'He keeps on ringing, he's driving me mad.
But I don't want to hurt him - I know he'll be sad'
She looked at me sideways and said 'I can't tell Dad,
He thinks Hugh's fantastic - the best boyfriend I've had.

'Hmm' I said pensively 'Well Hugh is a broker -
I've noticed he's boring and something of a joker.
He's going bald fast and he's not much of a 'looker''.
I'd assumed Sue loved his gifts and everywhere he took
    her.

Her face was pale, her eyes were red and she clenched
    her little hands
'Help me Mary, I'd help you, if there was someone you
    couldn't stand'
I thought of all the clothes she'd nicked, my black velvet
    alice band
The jeering as my latest spot stood loud and red and
    grand.

The telephone was sounding; concern for Sue grew
So I was the one to pick it up, take a breath and say
    'helloo?'
The tinny little voice whispered in my ear 'It's me. How
    are you?'
'I'm fine, who is this please? Oh, good afternoon Hugh'.

I found my strength and with head in the air
Said 'I'm sorry Hugh, I feel we're not getting anywhere.
'Oh' he laughed. 'I quite agree. You're not the one for me
    to marry
But I like your sister very much. Could you pass me on
    to Mary?'

Three Wise Men

'What's happened?' Norman asked himself for the umpteenth time. 'How on earth did I end up like this?'

Normally he would not allow himself the luxury of introspection, but this morning he had woken feeling unwell and quite unequal to the struggle of another day. It was early morning and still dark, so he reached up to the switch over his bed and turned on the light. He was cold and ducked back under the sparse bedclothes to keep the little pocket of warmth inside. He sighed and lay staring at the bare light bulb hanging undressed from the ceiling.

Norman was now 'on benefit' and glad to have any roof over his head. The landlady, Mrs Cox, was used to people like him – no-hopers, failures, people on the way down. She was not interested in him except as an occupant of one of her three bedsits, but she did not like the police coming round, so she made herself clear about trouble-makers, drunks, drug-users and prostitutes. Her accommodation comprised very little but then it cost very little to stay there.

Of course, Norman's life had not always been so difficult. He started off as an only, but much loved child of a middle class family. Both his parents were dead now and he was glad that they were not alive to see his misery. He had proceeded relatively well in his job with the insurance company, had married Barbara and fathered two children. When he realised that Barbara had been having an affair with his best friend over a long period of time, he succumbed to a nervous breakdown. When the divorce settlement was completed, Barbara, mainly because of the two children, was awarded the family home and almost all the rest of their assets as well as 75% of Norman" income. Not long after this, Norman was made redundant by his employer and had not been able to find employment of any sort since then. His disintegration had been fairly swift after this, which is why he now found himself in this sorry state.

He gazed up at the ceiling: 'Wouldn't it be lovely if this light-bulb radiated some warmth' he thought. 'I could pretend it does while I get dressed but I still have to force myself along to that filthy bathroom first – oh dear'. Poor Norman was a naturally fastidious man and simply dreaded the necessity of this shared facility. He reflected that the other occupants of this house must be in a very bad way to leave such mire behind them, but maybe it wasn't them at all, perhaps the bathroom was never cleaned at all by anybody and so it just built up.

Norman's bladder forced him out of bed, he put on his thin dressing gown and made his way along the corridor. Waiting outside the bathroom door stood another man; he was wearing an old striped bathrobe and looked as cold as Norman felt.

'Morning' they said at the same time.

Cedric had been waiting for five minutes already and he was keen to get on with the day. He had found a copy of The County Monthly in the street the previous evening and he planned to spend the morning looking for some sort of job. He too had experienced hardship but he was determined to keep fighting to regain his self-respect and his place in society.

Cedric smiled at Norman 'We must look a pretty comical pair standing her in the cold corridor waiting to use the filthiest bathroom in the world'.

Norman, who had not had an opportunity to talk to anyone for days, responded at once. 'I know, but we have to keep trying don't we? I am finding life very tough at the moment and don't know how to go forward from here'.

Cedric looked carefully at the other man. He was obviously from a decent background and his speaking voice reflected a steeper descent than most of the men in their situation.

'Hmm, you are in a bad way. Perhaps I can help? I found a copy of The County Monthly last night and thought I would spend the morning looking for something suitable. Perhaps we could team up and look together? Only thing is I have no light in my room at present and I know Mrs Cox has gone out so we would have to wait for her to return'.

Norman nearly laughed – something he had not done for a very long time. 'Well, I don't have much but you are very welcome to share my light bulb. I am in Room 3 so, when we are both washed and dressed, do come along and we can have a look together'.

At that point they heard the lock on the bathroom door being dragged back and, as Roy opened the door, a nauseating wave of urine and bleach reached them.

'Sorry about the stink chaps' chirped Roy. 'I have put some bleach around the place but it doesn't seem to have helped much – filthy place'.

'Well, at least you have tried, which is more than Mrs Cox seems to do' said Cedric and turning to Norman said 'see you in a little while then?' With a nod he stepped into the bathroom and closed the door.

'You two know each other then?' asked Roy.

'No, not at all, we've only just met. But whilst we were standing here we started chatting and realised that we're both in the same state in life so we thought we'd get together and have a look at Cedric's copy of The County Monthly this morning to see if there was anything we could do'. Norman smiled.

'My name's Roy' he said and held out his hand to shake Norman's. 'I'm at a very low ebb myself, and I wonder if you would consider letting me join you too. It's hard to admit but my desperation grows daily and I don't know how long I can keep going on like this with no hope'.

The two men looked at each other and both realised that there was no point in trying to pretend that their situations were different from reality – here they were and Cedric trying to get himself clean in the ghastly squalor of the room beside them.

'Please do join us' said Norman. 'We'll meet in my room, Room 3, because my light bulb is still working. I can't offer any hospitality though I'm afraid, I ran out of milk last night so I can't even make a cup of tea'. Cedric was delighted to be able to contribute something and said that he would bring along his pint of milk and they could have a nice cup of tea whilst they looked through the paper.

Later that morning, the three men, all cleanly shaved, dressed and well wrapped up, met in Norman's room. Roy and Cedric had brought their own mugs and Roy had his milk with him.

'Before we look into this' said Norman 'I wonder if we could have a think about perhaps teaming up – I have a background in insurance but the world went mad, my wife was unfaithful and I have lost everything. I don't feel sorry for myself but I should not have been so complacent about my life. I am relatively fit and actually like the idea of physical work. What about you two?'

Roy, a jovial type, told them that he had failed as a comedian. 'Always loved the idea of performing on stage, but simply wasn't good enough. I have been sliding down the scale for the last year and have trouble keeping my pecker up some days. You two have really cheered me up this morning'.

Cedric, it transpired had suffered from mental problems for years. 'I have been discharged into the community, whatever that means. Actually, I know what it means. It means, get out of here, get out of the way, stop being a nuisance and report to your social worker once a month. Sometimes I don't see any future at all, but I am really keen to try and make something of my life and I am physically strong, so let's see what's available'.

Whilst Roy and Cedric started looking through the pages, Norman made a cup of tea for them all.

The morning was taken up with discussions about various options for one or all of them. They did have somewhere to live after all, so they could move forwards and, with the support of each other, each felt stronger and more able to think ahead than they had when they woke that morning.

'Hang on a tick' said Roy 'What about this?' The three heads peered at the page where Roy was pointing.

'Don't be daft man' said Cedric 'this is the 'Business for Sale' section.

Roy looked excited and said 'I know, but think for a minute. This particular business for sale is a window cleaning business. What about approaching the owner and suggesting to him or her that we three start working in the business, and really build it up for them. Then later on, when we have earned some money, we could buy it?'

'I think we had better have another cup of tea' said Norman, trying not to show his excitement. The three men were all silent for a few minutes, listening to the hiss of the water boiling up in the kettle.

Finally, Cedric said 'I think this is certainly worth pursuing. You never know it might just be the thing and then we wouldn't have to live in this hellhole. Have you two still got some smartish clothes to wear? We don't want to go dressed for the city but we do need to look reasonable if we get a chance to meet the owner'.

'Yes, I have and a few spares if either of you need something; said Norman.

The men agreed that it should be Norman who made the first contact since he had a business background anyway. 'Yes, Good Morning. I am responding to your advertisement in The County Monthly. I wonder if it would be possible to arrange a meeting with you? My two business partners and I can be fairly flexible about time'!

A meeting was arranged for the following day, and the business was based in Archway, which was a ten-minute walk away.

Norman, Roy and Cedric spent the rest of that day with their heads together and practising different situation that might be encountered at the meeting such as awkward questions over current employment. Sometimes they laughed – Roy was really very funny and their spirits were high.

Mrs Cox returned to her house in the late afternoon and heard the noise coming from Room 3. She knocked on the door 'What's going on here' she demanded in her surly way. The years had not treated her well and a permanent scowl had settled on her jowly features. She was large and looked ready to throw a punch.

'Mrs Cox, how grand to see you' said Norman. 'Would you please arrange for something to be done about the heating in this room. I was nearly frozen solid when I woke up this morning'.

'I need a new light bulb in mine, thank you' said Cedric.

Mrs. Cox looked cross. 'I'll get round to it in due course, when I have a minute she snapped.

'No, no, no Mrs Cox' said Roy 'You really must look after us better than this. You see, we expect to be here for some time, maybe even six months. Things are looking up for all of us, and this, of course, is good news for you too'.

'We won't stay if you don't make the effort to see that we get value for money, will we?' Cedric chipped in. 'And whilst we are having this chat, Mrs. Cox, would you please arrange for something to be done about the bathroom? It really is quite disgusting. Roy here put some bleach about this morning but it needs a deep clean'. He gave her his best smile.

When Mrs Cox realised that three of her tenants had formed an alliance, that they were becoming friends and gaining strength individually, her attitude changed. She smiled, showing missing teeth 'Of course, gentlemen. I will see to these things at once.'

After she had gone, the three men looked at each other. How life can change – they had all started the day with feelings of hopelessness and despair, with little money and no perceivable future. They had pooled their resources and found fellowship and hope.

'Have we all got enough money to go and get some fish and chips to celebrate today?' asked Norman

.

Fashion

I bought a new outfit with my friend, Wendy
She said I was in danger of looking quite trendy.
The dress is made out of some fabulous stuff
And the hat a concoction of feathers and fluff.
The shoes, open toed will show polished neat feet
And my pearls will go with the whole thing a treat.
But, oh dear, I notice my bra and pants show
So with lots of advice to John Lewis I go.

Well, you cannot imagine the bras and the knickers
For every shape, size and naughty high kickers.
One poor solitary male stood amidst it all
Gazing steadfastly at the opposite wall.
His wife in a wheelchair was being advised
By one of those ladies whose looks testified
To her absolute knowledge of everything there
Challenge her? No, not me, I would not dare!

I hear they are comfortable, but belief I lack
I can't spend the day pulling string from the crack.
So the thongs stayed put and I wandered about
Looking for something flesh coloured and stout
I found them at last, just waiting for me
Plus the open-toed tights, a new mystery.

My husband will hate them and kick up a stink
Until he sees the finished article, a vision in pink!

Ancient Ken And Barbie

Both clearly shorter than they had once been – diminished by age. Barbie at 4' 10" wore a pale pink trouser suit, trimmed with a beaded braid. The clothes hung on defiantly although there was no longer a shape – no definition of her body. But her hair was still majestic! Thin now but a cascade of natural blonde surrounding a dainty, well-lined face where foundation lay in folds along the lines around her mouth and on her brow.

Ken leaned across the white damask cloth of their lunch table and, gazing earnestly at her, he smiled and said "We've got off to a good start" – having to repeat it several times in his mid-Western twang. He wore very pale blue – the same colour as his eyes, those eyes, which rarely left the face of this woman he clearly loves so much.

"Could we have something *frothy* to share?" Barbie asked the large Phillipino waitress. "We don't want much – just a little desert". Her voice was as soft as her faded curls.

And me, observing them, felt worried. Because both had that pallor, that 'end of life' look, with eyes that seem rimless and ever ready to see what is coming. Their fingers as they touched across the table, trembled slightly as though even that tiny contact would bruise their finger-ends.

Which one first? God willing - both together.

An Actor's Vowels

A   Alpha male

E   The only vowel of the second most important word –
ME

I   The most important word

O   Occupation – the most important

U   but never Non-U

Grief

I watch him grieve on those days when I come and offer
    him reprieve
From his endless watch over you
And he can hardly wrench himself away from his place
    by your side
Where he spends hours each day holding your hand and
    stroking your hair.
Your hair, once so lustrous and long, has become a dull
    grey
And they cut it short when they shaved that part of your
    head to
Slice and find the embolism that tried to take you.
The nurses – one is nearby round the clock - clip your
    nails,
Wash you and change your nightdress every day.
And they remove your soiled pads and monitor your
    heart.
Your poor darling heart.
I have tried to make you more fragrant, dabbing perfume
    on your wrists
But somehow, I can't seem to eradicate that awful smell
It's almost as though you are rotting from the inside
    outwards.

I try – I really do, not to recoil when I take my turn to
    feed you
And I always hope that I won't have to mop any food that
    re-emerges
Through your nose. It makes me retch.
My heart is broken because this is all that remains of you,
    my darling sister.
And I watch him grieve, this once powerful and strong
    man
And see the lines deepen on his brow and around his
    mouth.
The days of hopeful expectancy have passed and he has,
    finally,
Been forced to accept that he can never have you back
Excepting for the grunts and roars which are your only
    means of expression now
And which show him, in the only way possible, that you
    love him still.
How long must I watch him grieve?

My Moment Of Glory

I have just lost my job. It's upsetting to find your skills are no longer pivotal to an organisation, even if they have to make cuts. I knew that it would be difficult to find another job and that I probably faced long days feeling rejected and worrying about money.

However, I am resilient and, following various soothing words, I acknowledged that I had to do something to kick-start this next phase of my life. I felt the dawning realisation of what this should be flow over me in a smooth warm tide. I would stop walking past the fabulous window dressing of the famous milliner 'Crowning Glory' and go in. I would, out of my redundancy money, buy a gorgeous creation to cheer me on. A hat would be there at my behest. I could wear it whenever I chose.

I have always wanted to go to Royal Ascot – the Ladies Day in the Royal Enclosure in June. Perhaps I had never got over Audrey Hepburn as Eliza Dolittle. Each year I have recorded the occasion and revelled in the details: the arrival of the Royal party in carriages; the parade of beautiful racehorses in the paddock and, above all, the glamorous women in gorgeous feminine confections, the zenith of competitive dressing. Each year I made a small bet and nearly always lost, but I never cared, because I felt part of it all just for those few moments of the race.

I stood with brolly up outside my favourite shop in habitual London drizzle, looking carefully at the display and I saw what I wanted almost at once. Attracted by the festoons of pink roses, feathers and ribbon, the cerise brim angled over the sides that would frame my long chestnut hair. The sales assistant looked hesitant as she scanned my tired old raincoat but she helped me try it on and I bought it. I can't discuss the cost because I find breathing difficult when I do!

So, there I was on race day. That morning I had placed £50 on 'My Glory' running in the 4 o'clock with odds of 20/1. The bookmaker had looked pitying as he took my money - he couldn't know how relevant the name of the horse was!

I closed my curtains, put on a simple shift and my hat. I wore little make up but my hair gleamed in deep waves beneath my new love. The sun shone over Royal Ascot in a cloudless sky but I could see there was enough of a breeze to shift the flimsiest chiffon. I had rarely felt so excited.

As I sipped my way through a bottle of Cava, I watched and listened intently to everything on the screen. Time passed quickly and it was nearly 4 o'clock. I leaned forward, almost unable to control my trembling anticipation. Just like Eliza Dolittle, I found myself shouting encouragement and 'My Glory' did it. She won. Now I knew I could conquer the world.

Ode To A Washing Machine

YOU BEASTLY THING
YOU'VE EATEN ANOTHER SOCK!

Scandal Over Tea

Beattie's funeral was a terrific success – they all agreed.

Her final illness had been swift to conclude and her family and friends were grateful that Beattie only spent three days in the Hospice, comfortable and serene though she was, before succumbing to the invasion of cancer throughout her tortured frame.

'Dreadful for her boys,' hissed Joan to Charisse next to her. 'They're lovely people – I've known them all their lives of course.' This reinforced Joan's long-term importance to the family. Charisse sighed – she could have been just as involved if her husband hadn't taken her to live somewhere else.

The four old friends had met at Joan's house so they could travel to the church in one car. The ever self-effacing Molly insisted on climbing into the back sea with Charisse whose presence there was automatic, given her size. It took several minutes before the small car was loaded and then Irene announced that she ought to spend one last penny before they left. Eyes raised to the skies, Joan was glad they were so early.

All four in their early 80s, the ladies had all been born and raised in the Hertfordshire town of Tring. They'd gone to school together, coped with the war years, been bridesmaids at their weddings and enjoyed gossiping, frequently negatively with one or all of the remaining three, throughout their lives. Joan and Irene had continued to live in the town but Charisse had moved to the East End with her husband after the war, returning home after his death. Molly had gone wherever her job took her and ended up as Headmistress at a small Suffolk primary school, returning to her birthplace on retirement.

The church filled up quickly after the ladies had chosen their places, not too far back, but not in any of the pews marked 'Reserved.' 'After all,' squeaked Charisse, 'both Joan and Molly are regular church-goers.' In her ignorance she thought this gave them extra 'rights.'

Molly smiled her sweet patient smile, honed on children for thirty-eight years and Joan shrugged, her arms folded under the huge bosom so disproportionate to her short stature and slim hips.

Irene was already enjoying the service sheet and Charisse, sitting next to her, hissed her exclamation at the picture of Beattie. 'I bet that was taken twenty or more years ago,' she whispered loudly.

Joan, who'd had a perm that morning, was looking around to see who was there that she knew, turned her head quickly and muttered, 'For heaven's sake Charisse. Everyone could hear that.' She frowned with annoyance, wishing to disassociate herself from her friend's insensitivity.

The congregation stood as the procession started down the aisle. 'I am the resurrection and the life....' The Rector spoke loudly and clearly. As the coffin passed the four ladies, Joan felt a sharp elbow in her rib from Irene.

'That coffin's made of cardboard.' She said much too loudly for those around her. Joan and Molly both felt a mantle of embarrassment fall over them. 'Well I never.' Irene wouldn't be stopped, so great was her astonishment.

The Reception was in the church hall after the service. The four ladies, all wearing their best clothes, enjoyed the social occasion.

Joan said 'Shall we go for a drive after, then we can go to Westbury and have tea in that little café by the pond?'

Nodding enthusiastically at their stimulating day, they ate well and made a point of talking to Beattie's children. 'Hello my dear,' said Joan to just about everybody.

'She seems to know so many people,' Irene whispered to Charisse who said 'hmm' with her lips in a straight line. Joan had just interrupted their advance on an elderly man standing alone, sipping his tea.

Irene – with her regular disgruntled expression and a desire to turn all conversations back to her own misfortunes felt her usual wave of irritation. 'Why does Joan always have to be in charge?' she muttered under her breath and feeling cross that an opportunity to talk about herself with a complete stranger had been thwarted.

As always, Joan noticed the exchange, looking quickly away. She knew everything about Irene – how she had borne four children, but saw little of them – a natural 'sulker' and a demanding parent; she'd alienated them as children. Joan knew that most people found Irene profoundly annoying but theirs was a kind generation and clearly, this group of friends was a lifeline.

Irene gave a loud sniff and tried to change her expression. She felt certain that she and Joan, being the only two to remain in Tring without a break, gave their relationship the edge over the other two, she said nothing more, careful to maintain the status quo.

'I'll join you all in a minute' said Molly. 'I just need to check the lists'. Joan looked affectionately at the receding back of her old friend. Molly still had wonderful posture and exemplary dignity that Joan felt reflected well on the entire Parish.

'You're very quiet, my dear. Are you alright?' Joan asked Molly in her rear-view mirror.

The other two had been chattering away ever since they left the Wake, making appreciative noises about the bluebell wood as they passed and comparing it with the show in previous years, but Molly had hardly spoken.

A tall, angular woman she had never had any sort of close relationship with a man and had placed all her emotional energy into her job and then her faith. Both she and Joan were active members of their parish church and were often asked to act as sidemen for services. A reflective look had replaced her usual gentle expression so Joan knew that something was troubling her.

'Yes, I'm fine,' Molly smiled.

Charisse, who never missed anything, even when she was in the middle of a chat with someone else, looked speculatively at Molly beside her. Her sharp little eyes noted Molly's obvious disquiet and she hissed through her teeth in anticipation.

The ladies arrived at their destination and took a few moments to extricate themselves from the tiny two-door car. Charisse, whose original name had been Clarice had changed it in her thirties, after a film star. She stood close to Molly. Charisse, underweight and bird-like looked odd next to Molly's statuesque frame, but Joan, after locking her car, walked purposefully round and tucked her arm into Molly's

'Come on my dear – let's go and have tea.' She knew that she'd get Molly to talk and anyway it was her idea to come here and her car so she felt no hesitation in taking the lead. Charisse and Irene glanced at each other and shook their heads slightly, a conspiratorial look passed between them.

The tablecloth was the same as always – a thin gingham square over the plastic laminate. The crockery was pale green post-war utility stock that made them all feel comfortable and there was the familiar pleasant scent of fresh baking. Their table next to the window overlooked the village pond and a shaft of sunlight cast the shadow of the panes onto the table.

They ordered tea and scones and once done, the other three turned their faces to Molly.

'Come on then. Spill the beans.' Irene always hoped for some juicy revelation to titillate her. This time she was successful.

'I shouldn't really discuss this.' Molly said quite aware that she was going to anyway. 'I mean this is the way that gossip starts isn't it?' She looked at Joan who only nodded at her encouragingly.

Molly stayed silent for a moment whilst she inspected her neatly clipped nails, deep in thought.

'I'm very worried about the Rector,' she finally announced. 'When I left you before the service to go and find out whether I was needed next Sunday for 'sidesman' duties, I went into the Vestry and found the Rector and Julia Featherstone in ...' Molly was clearly struggling to describe what she saw.

'Ooh!' Charisse said in her two-tone way. Irene smiled broadly whilst Joan gazed at Molly intently.

Charisse's bright eyes gleamed and she was slightly flushed. 'Do you know what girls like Julia Featherstone are called?' she asked, looking at each of the other three in turn. Satisfied that she should continue, she said 'They're called Cock Teasers.' Both Molly and Joan dropped their chins onto their chests in dismay.

Irene hissed through her teeth with pleasure. 'Well, men are no better. They've always got something in their trousers they want to get out.' She laughed uproariously and even Molly who had never been 'with' a man was amused.

Their tea arrived and the elderly gentleman who delivered it was delighted to see four old ladies laughing so heartily. In his experience old ladies were often quite miserable things.

After the laughter subsided, Joan started to feel a bit piqued. She was certain that nothing would be 'going on' between the Rector and the attractive young woman, a regular communicant in the Church, but she liked to keep her finger on the pulse of her community. There wasn't much that got past her. She liked the Rector and his wife and resolved to make an appointment to see him so that she could tell him what had been seen, without mentioning Molly, and to warn him that gossip would almost certainly follow.

After clearing their plates, the four friends sat with their handbags on their laps waiting to pay their share. 'I think it would be best if none of us mentioned this thing that Molly saw to anyone else,' declared Joan. 'I'm sure there's a perfectly good explanation and we must be careful not to make trouble'.

Irene and Charisse nodded in agreement although both felt cross that such a juicy titbit was 'undiscussable' – well for the moment anyhow. Molly had sat quietly since making her statement, hating what she'd done and sad that she'd not only let herself down in her own eyes but in Joan's too.

'Home then?' asked Joan when the bill was settled and after yet another trip to the loo, each of them was folded into the small car and returned to their individual homes.

Joan walked briskly down the ramp with led to her front door. There was a chill in the early evening air and she was keen to get indoors. As she entered her house she could hear the beep of her 'answering machine'.

The male voice said, 'Hello Joan, this is the Rector. I need your help with one of our parishioners. I wonder if you'd mind ringing me when you get in. It's one of our ladies. Thanks. I'll wait to hear from you.'

Smiling contentedly, Joan went to put her kettle on. She could hardly wait to tell the other three that the difficulty they had discussed was now under control – hers.

Yearning For Him

I have watched him each day, every week all this year
From my desk in the corner, conscious of fear
Of discovery of my secret obsession, this burgeoning
    desire
For this man, so much older than I, but my heart is on
    fire.
And I want him to see me, to look in my eyes and know
I adore him. I want my emotion, my passion for him to
    show
But only this way, I'm quite shy, not a tart
He must traverse these blue windows into my heart.

Oh crumbs, it's the party – the annual office affair
When we all dress provocatively, and drink whatever's
    there
Oh God, his wife's with him and she looks very kind
I mustn't go near them, he must remain blind
To my everlasting ardour, but she will of course know
As soon as she sees me, and she'll tell him – I must go.
Going pink, sweating badly, trying hard to seem cool
I'm in serious danger of looking a fool.

'Don't go yet' I heard the beloved voice say
'Let's go and sit over there, where we're out of the way'

With heart pounding madly and wobbling knees
I allowed him to guide me through the door to the trees
Gathered swaying together in a copse by the lawn.
I felt helpless and hopeless, and saw that he knew
My naivete, inexperience – I really had no clue.
Smiling slightly he reached for me, and how I longed for
   this kiss
But with puckered mouth opened – yuck - he kissed like
   a fish.

The Man Cold

The world we now live in, unhappy to say
Is full of diseases, mal-nourishment, pain
There are those who watch helpless as their sons and
    daughters
Attempt to wash, cook and drink dirty green waters.

There are those who lie patiently waiting on pallets
P'raps with tubes in their arms and occasional tablets
To ease their departing from this mortal life
Caused by aids or neglect or famine or strife.

And then, there's the British bloke who's just caught a
    cold
His torment and anguish a sight to behold
With the first little tickle at the back of the throat
He starts to imagine survival's remote.

The sad little whine starts almost immediately
Seeking succour and comfort and undeserved sympathy.
"I'm sure this is bad and may turn to pneumonia"
It's so hard not to snap back with 'Just hypochondria'!

He starts shuffling about - his walk says it all
He has to lean on the furniture preventing a fall
Since his wobbly legs can't now take the strain
Checking to see if I'm watching, he's playing on his pain.

"Cough, cough" he begins, his mother's big sissy
"I really am worried this may turn to pleurisy"
I relent at last, 'cos he's being a bore
"Oops sorry darling, your temperature's high at 104.

He fights with himself, but his face shows the glee
Of justified comment on his agony
But it's tempered with something…. Could it be fright?
He's considering whether he'll last through the night.

As for me, I feel ghastly and everything hurts
But I know I'll feel better when I've ironed all the shirts,
Cleaned up the kitchen and hoovered all through
I can't be ill, I've got too much to do!

Together We Sorted It Out

We first met when I'd just turned fifty
Single mother of three, I had to be thrifty
But he had an income in excess of one-fifty
- So together we worked it out!

He had a house, paid for and furnished
Whilst my pad was rented and, in places, unfinished
And my chattels and goods - their value diminished
- But, together we worked it out!

My children still loitered, hoping for better
Whilst his had moved on with the occasional letter
at Christmas and birthday. He was unfettered
- Well, we soon sorted that out!

Dear reader – I suppose you think this one-sided?
That I took him because he had wealth undivided
But he wanted me with him, and once I'd decided
-     I knew we could sort things out!
-

It's right he had money and was very good looking
But he'd no one beside him to guard him and guide him
No warmth or attention, no real grass-roots loving
- I knew I could sort that bit out!

So here we are married, with no problems in view
And days' playing golf, bridge or trips to the zoo
And lovely long holidays, some grandchildren too
-    So, you see - together we sorted it out!

White Disk Of A Face

White disk of a face stared at me as it withdrew into the
    ether
Ethereal in the fading light of dusk
Definition of the heather became obscured in the
    twilight
And the mountains and streams quickly ceased to be
    visible.

Only a pale moon glowed in an otherwise deep black sky
And the headlights of the car before me from the back of
    which
The terrified tear-stained face of the boy had briefly
    emerged.
I had to be sure that my instinct was right. I had to
    follow.

Throwing my walking boots into the seat beside me, I
    placed
my stockinged feet onto the pedals before turning the
    switch.
The roar of the diesel abused the silence of this beautiful
    place,
but I could not worry about ecology at that moment.

It was a long way to the head of the glen
The track was deeply rutted in places but it was a car in
    front
And I had a land-rover which took the jolts
So the sickness I felt was anxiety. Did the child need
    help?

The creaky old wipers smeared the windscreen
As the drizzle began to intensify
And the road when we reached it shimmered
in the head-lights of the car in front.

The glow of habitation from the village came into view
And I longed briefly for the hit of cold beer to the back of
    my throat
when the pub lights gentle radiance loomed ahead.
My surveillance car slowed then pulled into the
    forecourt. So then did I.

Padding round to the boot to find shoes, my socks were
    soon wet
And the leather squeaked as I forced my feet into place. I
    watched.
The mother carefully lifted the small sleepy boy and
    carried him
covered with a blanket into the welcoming front door.

I understood my mistake but in this world of troubled
    children
I felt no shame in following my instinct. I have little ones
    of my own.
'Is he OK?' I asked after giving my order after theirs.
'Yes, he is now' smiled the father. 'He saw the end of
    Cleopatra yesterday

so, seeing a snake today, was too soon'.
We smiled and raised our glasses in salute.
'Thank you for your concern' said the mother smiling
    into my eyes
'It was good of you to make sure'.

The Gold Watch

I can't find my mother's gold watch. It's the one with worn link chain and the slight dent in the back of the casing. I was handling it the other day and wondering whether I should sell it since the price of gold is so high at present, or whether it had more value as an antique. I want some money stashed away. I would not have thrown it away and I would, surely, only have put it in a separate box, like my own trinkets.

Suddenly, perhaps from a great distance, I heard her well-remembered laughter. I felt confusion and regret, then sorrow quickly followed by amusement.

'I've hidden it' she cackled in that tone which reminded me of my status as one of her second class children. After a few seconds I heard her sigh – maybe regret of her own? I felt the twitch of my mouth as she triggered an involuntary smile from me because, even in death and so far apart, there has grown an established love between us and I knew that, eventually, I would find her gold.

Adultery

The evocative scent of dried dampness on the life-jackets normally stowed in the bow locker, mingled with the breeze sweeping across the loch. The little boat chugged noisily, lifting and dropping rhythmically over the grey surface. They were being taken to see the salmon farming operation at the western end where the current flowed at the point nearest to the sea. The weekend in Scotland for the group of eight had been planned for nearly a year.

The three women sat under the semi-shelter of the plastic canopy. Fiona looked carefully at her friend, Joan. She noticed the lines of strain, evident after the chemotherapy, still etched around her eyes and the thinning white hair blowing across the dear face, even though it was supposed to be contained in the waterproof hood of her red jacket.

Aware of scrutiny, Joan smiled and straightened her spine, forgetting the confines of the fibreglass wheelhouse. 'What?' she asked softly, unwilling to be overheard – it was too soon.

Kate leaned in to listen but there were no further words just small smiles and the slapping of the water.

Later, as they all stood around talking over drinks before dinner, Fiona heard Kate take a sharp intake of breath and looked to see what had caused it. It was the level of intimacy in the embrace between Joan and Fiona's husband, Tom.

Tom sat next to Joan at dinner and Fiona watched them, as she knew Kate was.

'Everything all right, old girl?' bellowed Joan's husband Mike 'You seem very quiet these days'.

'No, I'm fine' Fiona responded but she knew she wasn't.

There had been months of barely speaking to each other and never touching between her and Tom. She had continued to hope that he would realise how much he had hurt her and try to put things right. Looking at him now, she realised the finality of her situation. Their marriage was over.

Tom looked across the table at Fiona; he was smirking and clearly rubbing Joan's knee under the table. 'Having a nice time Darling?' he called.

Suddenly, Joan rose to her feet 'Well, I'm not – Kate would you mind changing places with me? I think I'm in a draught'.

When Joan had settled in her new place, she leaned towards Fiona and said loudly 'How's my very best friend in the whole world then?'

The two women smiled at each other. 'You will help me won't you?' whispered Fiona.

'Always' said Joan.

Comfort Zone

'Get out of your comfort zone' was the first thing I heard
'Not likely' I thought 'How completely absurd -
I have only attained this nice presence of mind
After years of endeavour, I am quite disinclined
To take on this nonsense of how it should be
If you wish to take part in their prosperity.

It's an MLM outfit if you know what they mean
With wonderful products that nourish and clean
Every part of your body, every bit of your house
And there's no other company with the right sort of
        nouse
To support you, exhaust you, exhort you to more
When you finally wonder who on earth its all for.

I had to conclude after giving my best
To support my beloved, but my word what a test
Of our wonderful marriage, and I came to see
That the right way forward for my husband and me
Was to put energy, laughter, commitment and time
Sitting here at the computer writing this rhyme!

David With The Head Of Goliath Painting By Caravaggio

A view

No one could question your Ability
The use of darkness, the blessing of light
Images captured for all eternity
Reveal holy moments, holiest might.
Goliath slain with minimal difficulty
Severed head aloft, after the fight
By David whose face is pure serenity
Untainted innocence draped in white.

But the Giant's face is yours, a record of strife,
Testimony of violence in your own life.

Dorothy Ellen
A tribute to my Mother-in-Law

Many women sometime have a mother-in-law
They can be charming and helpful or a complete crashing
    bore!
They can sit with pursed lips - criticise what you do
With your children, her son – and your virtues are few
so it seems in the atmosphere tense she creates
with her sniffing and sighing and heart full of hate.

But let me tell you about **my** mother-in-law
Who kept her mouth tight shut, whatever she saw!
Her hairline had horn holes at the front of her style
like Elizabeth, Her Majesty, who has the same smile.
She wore pink or blue twin-sets, completed by pearls
And tweed skirts and brogue shoes, the ones made for
    girls.

Her life had been hard, though I never met her spouse
But I heard that he gambled and drank much 'Old
    Grouse'
He'd died early and left her with a mortgage to pay,
A ramshackle garden, debts and a '57 chevrolet.
Plus four rugby boys and their 'brylcreamed' hair -
Competitive, boisterous and reluctant to share.

That instant rapport, exclusive hers and mine
Echoed through the years and my own trying time.

Oh how I valued that lilting Welsh voice
And the laughter, the recipes and other advice.
She died suddenly, too early, and I grieved for a while
But say 'Dorothy Ellen' and it will always make me
    smile.

Fantasy – Supper On The Beach

The companion was nameless when I first hatched this
    plan
Actually faceless, unknown to me, but clearly a man.
I sat in the warmth overlooking the sea,
With a book, plate of biscuits and a nice cup of tea.

As my gaze ranged as far as the horizon beyond
I was lost in my reverie and the wind in the fronds
Of the palm trees above me didn't bother me then
I was thinking of laughter, good music and men.

The most perfect setting for a new love affair
Was down there on the beach where the wind in my hair
Would make me look wilder, a cat on the prowl
Sitting there near the cliff on my bright yellow towel.

I'd be brown skinned and slim in an elegant sarong
And hope that my legs just looked endlessly long
Through the silk of my garment with nothing below
Except tiny lace panties which I'd make sure did show!

The food is all ready – I've got fresh bread and brie
Lobster, salad and peaches with an ice cold Chablis.
The shellfish needs breaking and I have a sharp knife
Feeling reckless and giggly – it's the time of my life.

'Here, let me' says the man and with one swift knock
On the knife on the fish with a flat sided rock
Cuts the lobster in half, red and white fleshy meat
Succulent and delicious - we're ready to eat.

Bohemian picnic, we eat with our hands
And the juices unchecked run from chins into sand
Our eyes do not stray from the eyes of the other
And we laugh for we know that we'll finish as lovers.

The epoch starts its first journey from day into night
We watch, leaning together, to see the green light
Flash as the sun dips its final bright beam
On this fabulous setting, this heaven – my dream.

Gnarl

I've noticed a lump on my finger
The little one last on the left
And I'm trying not to malinger
Or feel totally, utterly bereft!

You see - I'm almost sure it's a gnarl
A revolting lump on the bone
Which arrives like an unwanted pearl
To other women – those we call crones!

I have tried over months to ignore it
Quite sure that something so foul
Could not possibly happen to one with such wit
As me. A woman with so much soul!

Dammit!

My Friend's Fellow

My friend Patricia has a new fellow
He smokes, so he stinks and his teeth are quite yellow
His nails are all bitten and so are the edges
You can see crusting scabs round his benson and hedges
He's short and quite stout with thinning grey hair
And brown trousers with stains and a hint of a flair.

'Is she so desperate?' I thought as I watched
He, shouting on his mobile and she with her cloth,
wiping the dishes from the freshly cooked meal
of asparagus and salad with beautiful veal.

Her mother called round whilst I was there
We both fought not to notice and tried not to stare
As this specimen stroked 'Tricia low on her bum
Making it clear this was now one on one!

Pat's Mum looked at me and I looked at her
Our looks said the same thing - the look said 'Oh dear'
Woman to woman our glances disclosed
Our common dismay at the one Pat had chose.

With your children you know not to show your reaction
But this is my dear friend and I must take some action
I said 'Do you have children? Been married before?'
He replied 'Yes, thirteen children, but wives only four'.

Pat's mother sat down with a crash on her chair
She had paled and was frantically moving her hair
In her desperate attempt to regain equilibrium
As I raked through my bag, searching for 'valium'.

'It's my life' whispered Pat from her mutinous chin
'You both tell me I'm lonely, looking anxious and thin.
Well Trevor's my answer. I don't care what you say.
He's kind and considerate and so helpful today.

Then tomorrow we're off on a cruise to the med
So goodbye both, we're tired now and ready for bed.
We left them, embarrassed, Pat's mother and me
I was quite rattled and so, clearly, was she
Pat's Mum looked at me and I looked at her
Our looks said the same thing - the look said 'Oh dear'.

Derelict Bricks

Across the road, set well back in a dip in the land
Stand the dilapidated remains of a once proud home
What had she been like, the woman whose hands
Would have nurtured and cleaned until her old bones
Gave up on her and she succumbed, as we all must
To the dirt she had fought, to be buried in dust.

What a waste, I do think, to have spent all your youth
Cooking and cleaning, tending the beasts
Not looking for beauty, nor seeking the truth
But preparing, out of nothing, an evening feast.
I hope she was happy and that, somehow, her life
Wasn't as bad as I think it – filled with hardship and
    strife.

The roof has gone down, doors, windows have rotted
Whilst today's tractor cultivates up to the edges
Of a patch where geese, ducks and chickens maybe
    strutted
near a once well-cared for garden with neat hawthorn
    hedges.
I'm aware of her spirit though; her voice can be heard
Notwithstanding the elder and ivy and old man's beard.

An American Woman

You're plump and smooth with blonded hair, lips fuller
    than your start
A sense of spoiled indulgence is all you do impart
No scowl will crease your creaseless brow, your face it
    does not move
It cannot since the surgery that eradicated grooves.

Body language is also fierce, breasts pert but shoulders
    rigid
Unmoving to a greeting called – You're unpleasant,
    nasty, frigid
So, Mrs American – Are you pleased? Are you top of the
    range?
For to me you're scarcely human, not attractive, really
    strange.

Is that expression of yours hostile or superior?
So hard for anyone to tell from the static and cold
    exterior.
Now, as I stare I can see that you're pleased and think
    yourself lovely
But to me, your observer, you have MADE yourself
    weird and actually ugly.

Foreign Attraction

The silver vaults were in the basement of the stately home. The aisles were close-carpeted, softly lit and quiet except for the subdued murmuring of the visitors.

Mia had noticed on her way in that the doors were steel, heavy and as thick as the length of her forearm. The display cabinets were clearly wired up with double thickness glass and there was a regular patrol of two security guards, both of whom looked disconcertingly alert.

Clutching at the literature she had been given at the entrance and which now felt warm and familiar, Mia reminded herself that all of this wealth belonged to the March family – and had done for over four hundred years.

She stood alone at the furthest end of the vault from the entrance and gazed at the spectacle in front of her. Solid gold dishes and goblets, tureens and cutlery were displayed on dark blue velvet and, at the centre, was one large punch bowl encrusted around the rim with diamonds, emeralds and rubies. Peering closely, Mia detected the crest of the March family on every item, including the smallest teaspoon.

For Mia Tsung-lee this was her first experience of exhibited personal wealth. Wearing jeans and a sweater, she stood with her sandaled feet set apart and her hands, still holding the paper, behind her back underneath her small backpack. She wore her long black hair in a ponytail and her oriental eyes shone with desire. She licked her parted lips and left her tongue protruding slightly from one side of her mouth in a gesture of concentration.

Nothing in her background could have prepared Mia for the feelings that now swept over her. Rage, resentment and a sickening lump of hopelessness settled in her stomach. She continued to stand quite still as she considered her situation again. Gradually her eyes became unfocussed.

The day had started quite well and she had woken next to Jason in her own bed at the hostel. She felt optimistic and looked forward to receiving the news which she was sure would arrive to tell her that she'd done well in her first year exams and could, therefore, stay in the UK. She'd been waiting for several days and knew that most of her friends had received their confirmation of places for continuing education. Her notification had arrived that morning, but it wasn't an offer at all – instead she was told that she had not done well enough in her first year exams even to be considered for retaking them. This meant that her student visa would be invalid and she would have to leave the United Kingdom imminently.

In retrospect she saw that the excitement of being in England, the different culture, the lack of restrictions and the opportunities available had been too brilliant to overcome. She simply hadn't worked hard enough in her first year. But this summary dismissal seemed harsh to her and she still felt tearful and upset, although she didn't blame anyone but herself.

Mia thought of Jason waiting for her outside. He would, she knew, be sitting reading his book in his battered old car with his trainers on the dashboard. He'd brought her here to try and change the subject, he'd said. After an hour or so, he told her that he realised that maybe it wasn't such a brilliant idea to bring her to view something which epitomised so clearly the history and wealth of the country whose nationality she craved and which had rejected her.

'Poor little thing. I'm really sorry.' He'd said.

They had toured the main house together and she understood his growing frustration at her continued silence and lack of response.

'Best to leave her on her own for a while,' was his relieved conclusion and he left her to it. He had a good book anyway.

Mia stayed in the vaults for a long time. She scrutinised the treasures individually and wondered who had made them, where they came from and whether or not their owners were as interested in them as she was. She thought about how much they might be worth.

Finally, she heard a bell and one of the security guards was bearing down on her and politely asking her to leave since they were about to shut the house.

Once back in the car beside him, Mia started to tell Jason how she felt. Although they had spent a lot of time together at university and she had visited his home in leafy suburbia, he didn't really know what sort of background she came from.

Naturally reserved and unwilling to expose her humble origins against his, she had said little. Consequently she now had his full attention.

She said, 'It's not fair that I have to be sent back to Taiwan; back to my life of dreary poverty without the education that my father saved so hard to buy me, in disgrace and alone. I don't know how I'll face him or the rest of my family. I'm the first one that has ever had this opportunity and they were all so excited and proud of me. They thought that, with this chance, my future would depend on my own success and so my failure doesn't just affect me.' An emotional hiccup escaped from her throat. I suppose,' she continued, 'a nice husband will be found for me eventually and I'll then have a life of babies and cleaning and cooking. All this facing me when in there…' and she jabbed her finger back at the house, 'they have treasures so important and so beautiful that even one small object would probably be enough to buy me the rest of my life in England or somewhere in the West. I love it here and desperately want to stay.'

Jason was always captivated by Mia's traditional use of English words and her 'lispy' accent, but suddenly, to his horror, she broke down and long wracking sobs echoing from deep inside her chest rose to join the cascading tears falling unchecked down her cheeks.

Jason had been about to turn the ignition of his old car but he turned to her at once and, within the confines of the two front seats, he tried to take her in his arms. The gear stick and handbrake lever made his movements difficult but anxious to comfort her as best he could, he persevered.

'Oh dear, Mia. I hate to see you like this.' He said.

She responded by holding her flat little face up against his proffered chest and his shirt became wet with her tears.

Jason, apart obviously from his mother, came from a big family of boys, and was completely baffled by feminine distress, particularly at such close quarters. He tried to stop himself from providing a rigid pair of arms and hands, but his awkwardness transmitted itself to Mia and she pulled herself upright, whilst giving a large sniff and wiping her nose delicately with the back of one hand.

Feeling glad that he could obviously offer Mia his hankie, Jason started rooting around in his jeans which were too tight to get his hand in his pocket from this sitting position. But, after a certain amount of manoeuvring and stretching he managed to pull a tired old rag out and proffered it to her.

She laughed. The sunshine of her smile after the recent spell of wetness on her face arrested him completely. Before he gave it any thought at all he said in a quick and high-pitched tone:

'Mia, I really love you, I think. I don't like the idea of you leaving and I wonder if you would be allowed to stay if we got married?'

Shocked, they stared at each other for some minutes and then, in complete unison, they turned to look out of the window away from each other.

The Adam's apple in Jason's throat gave a great dive and he started to shudder.

'You great pillock,' he chastised himself, 'there's one thing finding a girl as attractive as Mia and quite another to jump into the future like this.' He peered at her profile – so different to his. He'd always been impressed by oriental girls as he found them so feminine and dainty, so responsive and willing in bed. An English girl, he imagined, would have come back with some pithy sarcasm, but this little one just sat there gazing out of the window, unblinking and sad.

'I would make you a good wife Jason,' Mia said quietly, 'but I don't think this is a good idea. We have too many difficulties. We have no money and my father would not continue to support me if we got married; we have nowhere to live and our cultural differences are so great. Also….' And she looked at him sadly, 'I think you are only saying this because you feel sorry for me.'

His relief showed. He realised that everything she said was true and felt grateful to her that she hadn't jumped at his offer.

'Crikey,' he thought, 'Mum and Dad would have gone ballistic..'

Jason took Mia's little hand in his. 'What can I do to help you? Can you think of anything?'

She looked at the earnest face before her. She really did like Jason and he'd been a good friend during the past year. He'd been her first lover and had treated her with gentleness and courtesy. She understood that he was relieved that she hadn't accepted his offer and felt a momentary pang of regret at her quick decision.

Through the trees in the twilight, Mia glanced back towards the stately home.

'Do you mean it Jason? Would you really help me with something?' Mia looked so hopeful that the young man had to concentrate on keeping a straight face and as he nodded his assent the usual lock of hair fell forward onto his deep brow.

Mia turned back towards the house and he suddenly realised what she was going to ask him to do.

She said, 'Just one little tiny object would make the biggest difference to the rest of my life, wherever I am. Will you help me? Please?'

He didn't believe that she was serious until he searched her face and saw her nodding encouragingly at him for an affirmative response. 'No. Absolutely not.' Jason was both embarrassed and annoyed. He started the car and drove off into the deepening gloom of the evening.

They were silent on the journey home, and were both glad of the radio. After two hours he pulled up outside the building in which she lived and she stepped out of the car without looking at him and ran up the stairs to the front door without saying a word. She didn't even say Goodbye.

He knew that he would never see her again.

Menopause And Other Feminine Trials

What has this to do with the men of the world?
It should just be 'Opause', 'struation' and pre-strual.
They've got in on the act, and just won't be told
That it's boring, embarrassing and painful as well.

Hot flushes that make you red, dewy and hot
The anxiety of flooding - you're too nervous to sit
The upper chin beading, exposing that spot
And those circles of sweat seeping under each pit

'It's the 'change' love' he says, 'we can look forward at
    last
To no more contraception, no pills, caps or durex.
How thrilling to think with the working life past
We can spend all our waking hours enjoying free sex!'

Groan – another damn thing to cope with it seems
He thinks it's so helpful to make it seem light
He's convinced I'll return to the woman of his dreams
But the fact is the bugger's been snoring all night.

I'm exhausted, frustrated with feeling so low
But the positive side of my nature, I know

Will return one day when this ordeal is through
And the hormonal chrysalis breaks through to show
The saggy flesh, collagen, hips widely spreading
To the next phase, the one I know we're all dreading
That of old woman, the granny, the sage
The ghastly appearance of feminine old age.

And Finally = AMEN!

The Piece Of Grass

I watched the clump of sod fall from the bank into the
    eddy
And one long piece of grass taken, just a single stalk
Separated from the rest to wave frantically and then
    steady
As the current held it away from the clay and the chalk
That had been its home since its first peep of green
Had appeared early in May, a sight unobserved by human
    eye.
But of interest perhaps to everything that lived by the
    stream
That scratched or slithered and fought in their quest to
    stay alive.

That blade of grass, or so it seemed, had a similar
    problem to you and me
With no input as to where or when, how or why
It would be created, and with what genes, when it came
    to be.
It just got put there; seed blown on the breeze and will
    forever try
To reinforce its roots and stay in this difficult place on
    the edge

Surviving each little flood, each lashing storm with
    torrential rain
The trampling by the farmer's dogs which run through
    the hedge
Disinterested, and unaware of the fight and the bruising
    pain.

I often think of that small blade of flora, spellbound by
    fragility
Eroded by each swirl and passing debris until finally it
    must let go
As must we all. But into what - because I don't believe in
    finality
And no one anywhere, any time, any place can persuade
    me this isn't so.
I reject that life's meaning is transitory, purposeless and
    futile
Or that we have no say in our lives hereafter, or what
    comes to pass
And I'm quite sure that it's worth spending a while
Returning to dwell on that small blade of grass.

Yorkshire Beer

Florence is her name, the same as her mother
But say 'Mrs Braithwaite' so as not to offend her
This stalwart barmaid, this Yorkshire specimen
A true caricature of Northern women.

Locals know this bar well, geographically placed
A hostelry large enough to be royally graced
Says a plaque indicating that Victoria was there
Near to the main station in Hull's central square
It's a haven for travellers as they step off the train
Before going home in the wind and the rain.

Two fragile men, just wanting a beer
On approaching the bar there was nobody there
They shuffled their feet and shared furtive glances
Should they move on, or wait on their chances?
One lost heart and took a step back
Just as the bar plank closed with a snap
And slowly, so slowly as she raised her eyes up
The old barmaid moved forward, picked up her cup
Of cold tea that had waited forlorn by itself
Next to her 'daily' on sticky plastic shelf.
She sniffed with disgust at the taste of her drink
And waddled to throw the remains in the sink.

'Well, whady'a want' she glowered at the smaller
who puffed his chest out and tried to look taller.
Was he pushed about by old women like this?
Feeling flustered and hot, his two hands in a fist
He opened his mouth but nothing came out
So he tried a bit harder and decided to shout
But the noise he had hoped for was no more than a
     murmur
And clearing his throat, he managed to stammer:
'Two pints of bitter please' and felt his hand rummage
inside his pocket, but all he could manage
was to tip the lot out, dirty hanky and money,
betting slip, vick inhaler and some well chewed gummy.

The scarred tepid glass hit the bar and slopped over
So splattering the fiver that the man hoped would cover
The cost of his nectar and that of his friend
Who'd sloped off to a table, unwilling to defend
Himself or his host from this horrid behaviour
Because at the end of his day of honest endeavour.
He didn't need to endure – he just wanted the foam
Off the top of his beer to tickle his throat before he went
     home.

Mrs B. flung the change into the puddle of beer
Whilst glaring and swearing, but her victim didn't hear
Since he'd snatched up his pennies and hastily moved
To the side of the room where the ambience improved.
The two men looked at each other and gave a small smile
As they lifted their elbows. It had been worthwhile.

Ode To A Boaster

I introduced my husband to my best friend Alison's lover
They shook hands and looked carefully from one face to
    the other
Mine circled, eyes assessing as many male species do
To calculate his interest in this stranger, although few
Rose to meet his demanding expectation of how one
    should behave
Starting with his fixed idea that every man should shave.
From over his tawny beard, kind blue eyes gazed back
Understanding completely the other man's lack
Of genuine interest in who he was, from where or why
And he smiled when he registered the other man's sigh
As he launched himself into his favourite theme
Of how well he had done, how he'd lived his dream.
I squirmed as I listened to the oft-told tales
Of escape from the valleys of industrial Wales
How he'd conquered the enemy in foreign lands
And struggled to survive in Arabian sands
With medals to show for his outstanding past
My beloved held forth, until at last
He said to the other man in a tone supercilious
'So, what's your life's work been – anything serious?'
I heard Alison snigger at this negative query

And the answer: 'I'm a doctor – plastic surgery…'
'Ho ho' said my husband delighted to think
this person's rich clients came along with their shrinks
for more pampering, indulgence and expensive therapy
'Well' he drawled. 'I expect you make women happy'.
'No, you don't understand' the doctor replied
I knew what his job was and I wanted to hide
'I treat children with scars of war or genetics -
they fly in from all over. I'm in paediatrics.'

Single Mother Of Boys

What on earth can you say to your son of 13
Who thinks his willy's different to others he's seen
He's come to believe he's deformed, unlike others
Including my other two - his older brothers.

Face twisted with anguish, anxiety, sorrow
This can't wait another hour, never mind tomorrow
'I'm not going to look love, it wouldn't be right,'
I try to soothe him and he stares back in fright.

'How about asking the others I mean Tom and Dick?'
His head shakes emphatically, he said he felt sick.
It's the first time in years that I've thought of his Dad
Who should've been here, now, supporting his lad.

Still, we've been okay without him, we've done really
    well
And I'd heard that his next wife put him through hell.
We all make mistakes, sometimes causing great pain
His loss is enormous with no permanent gain.

My darling child gazed at me, waiting for action
From the one he loves most, which isn't a fraction
Of the way that I feel about him. Oh dear what can I do?
Inspiration hits suddenly. 'I'll ring Dr. Shaggoo.'

The Surgery Receptionist icily states
That the Doctor is busy and I'll just have to wait
Which I do with that young face searching mine
Checking for worry, concern or any other sign.

'I'm sorry to keep you. Can I help you at all?'
It's my wonderful doctor answering my call.
After listening he chuckles 'Send him round and I'll wait.
But don't let him tarry, I'm tired and it's late.'

The wonderful Scot with his name of Shaggoo
Became my friend years ago, when out of the blue
We met through a friend when my feelings still raw
Showed and he knew I was frightened, lonely, insecure.

What a friend he has been and today's no exception
My little lad reappeared, smiling, clear-complexion
'I'm normal, Mum. It's all quite okay.'
Then he laughingly asked me 'What's for supper today?'

We all need encouragement, reassurance, support
And till now I've managed, in spite of the fraught
Situations encountered with three lively boys
Their alien humour, testosterone, toys.

The kit's been an ordeal with the familiar smell
Of wet mud and BO, the socks stink as well
Testimony to masculine pursuits of rugby or cricket
Ah those green stains on whites earned whilst chasing a
    wicket.

My background is feminine, I wasn't used to males.
I always thought they were noisy things, inclined to tell
    tales.
Then of course I fell for one and we agreed to marry

And I ended up as a single mum to Tom, Dick and Harry.

The Cake

Delia said that this perfect sponge is the easiest thing to
    make
She said 'mix all the ingredients together, whisk and
    bake.'
So, why is it always me that ends up with a biscuit affair
With rock solid round things to front and to rear?
The jam doesn't help, I made it myself – what a star
Until now I discover it won't leave the jar!
Well I'm fed up with it now and I've told my old man
To sharpen his fangs and do what he can.

The Vase Of Affection

The bouquet starts assembling immediately. The child is born and, usually, there are two parents who place their strong stems in the pure water of the vase. Soon there will be others – Grandparents, Uncles and Aunts, maybe brothers or sisters. This is the perfect start for the best arrangement.

As time goes by other, weaker blooms will take their place in the still clear waters of the vase and the child will learn to trust those who have placed themselves in that confection of scents, textures, colours and softness. These are all adults.

Eventually this person will choose to invite others to join their 'arrangement' and this is when the waters can start to cloud. A small girl could say 'You were my best friend, but I hate you now' and two vases will shudder on their metaphorical shelves. A small boy may grieve over exclusion from a team and a leaf might drop to the bottom to rot slowly.

But adolescence is a time for collecting multiple-flowering heads, from school, work-experience, college, holidays and finally the first job.

The vase sits quietly waiting and the spirit of the child as it has grown kept the water clear with innocent optimism and pure expectation.

Time passes and some of the original flowers have died and been removed, their shadows lingering in essences around the water line.

Eventually the strongest bloom of all – a dark, deep velvet red rose provides the backbone for all the others around it and there it should stay holding everything together as the rest of the original flowers die and have to leave.

Beware of evaporation, of the gradual dismantling of affection, of the disillusions that come from this perfect age of selfishness and greed for things that do not matter.

Keep your vase clear of weeds and unwanted intrusion and invite only those flowers who have gained your trust with love and loyalty and never allow plastic or artificial horticulture anywhere near.

Country House Hotel Tea

Lee picked up a copy of Country Life from the table in front of him. It seemed the least daunting and the thinnest magazine of the selection. As he opened it he could smell the quality of the paper and rubbed his rough fingers over the smooth surface.

'Listen to this' he shouted out. Once he knew he had their attention he continued:

'A picture here of The Hon. Samantha Barslow (also known as Samba)' he was interrupted by Dawn.

'That's a dance you know' she smiled smugly and tucked her folded arms underneath the magnificent bosom.

'I thought it was a snake' said Denise.

Lee looked irritated and shook the magazine slightly to indicate that he was ready to resume reading the piece. 'Dance or snake, it doesn't matter. Anyway she's going to marry someone really important apparently. I think she looks just like a horse', and he threw his head back and laughed heartily.

The waiter wheeled in the tea trolley. Denise rose instantly to her feet and started to rattle the cups and saucers. The waiter gently took them from her.

'Sit down' rapped Madge sharply.

As Denise lowered herself stiffly back onto her chair, Madge leaned towards her and hissed.

'For heaven's sake. I know you aren't used to this but do you have to let it show?'

Denise rifled through her bag looking for a kleenex. She hoped not to start crying but she couldn't count on it.

'Ow would you lake your tea Madame?' Denise stopped her search and stared at the French waiter.

Opening her mouth to say 'Hot and wet' Denise was interrupted by Madge who spoke imperiously 'Strong with milk and two sugars for her please and the same for me. My husband likes it slightly weaker and with no sugar'.

Lee very slowly lowered his magazine and looked menacingly at Madge. 'In your dreams Dearie' he muttered.

The porcelain cake-stand was crowded with tiny cakes and pastries; the sandwiches were thin and crustless and the odour of warm scones dominated the table. Clotted cream oozed in a crystal dish and whole strawberries lazed in the jam.

'Got a very small plate to put that lot on' Denise complained.

'Just one thing at a time, starting with the sarnies' suggested Lee.

The trio munched their way through the whole lot and didn't register the waiter's amazed expression when he returned to clear away.

'Well' said Lee leaning back and patting his firm beach-ball of a stomach 'I thought that was the nicest meal of my life. What a lovely present to give us. I must say, that Mrs Wells does know how to look after her staff. Come on Ladies; let's get home. I'll need to polish the car before the theatre trip. You got a night off Denise?'

'Yeah. They won't need feeding tonight but there'll be plenty of cleaning up for you to do Madge. I'll give you a hand if you like?'

Lee, Denise and Madge put on the coats that were retrieved for them. They gazed wistfully around the great hall with the vast stone fireplace; the ancestral portraits; the massed collection of orchids on the centre table. They breathed in the scent of wealth.

'It's so lovely here, I do hope we can come back another day' said Madge quietly.

'I think that's up to us, don't you?' Lee whispered through his grin.

An Interesting Mind

Say what you will, whether horrid or kind
But you can't get beyond an interesting mind
It garners and stores all that is known
And perhaps nothing on the outside lets it be shown.

It's said that everything is written on an older face
All the lines and wrinkles have taken their place
Because of movement often repeated
Whether smiles or frowns from moments heated.

Skin will react to smoking and drinking
And lying in sunshine without ever thinking
About exposure to all those bad rays
Caught spent outside in youthful days.

A body will thicken and the hair may grow thin
Outside disasters don't reflect what's within
Spectacles might hide the depth of reflection
And hearing aids deepen deaf introspection.

You don't have to be old to be granted this grace
I have known children with innocent face
From two to sixteen with little life experience
Respond heedless of adult rules or deference.

It's a sort of phenomena, a natural commodity
Which can't be inherited or acquired by the laity
Priests and clergy understand this quality
And strive to secure it throughout their ministry.

So hard to describe an interesting mind
It's wide-ranging, intuitive, selfless and kind
Emotional, intelligent, always willing to grow
And if you're lucky to have one – well you already know.

From Booze To Eternity

Caroline lay on the floor where she had slid off the chair several hours previously. The duvet that had been placed over her hadn't moved. As usual she was unhurt but annoyed that her weak cries had been ignored. As she lay there the same thoughts came to her, as they did every day when she awoke, wherever that might be, and her feelings of deep resentment were never appeased.

Hearing her daughter's footsteps on the landing, Caroline gave a little smile of pure malicious joy and urinated where she lay.

Claire had woken early and her natural reaction to the start of a beautiful day was immediately banished when she remembered that her mother still lay on the Dining Room floor.

Claire turned over and gazed at her husband who was still asleep. James didn't look his best. His mouth was open and he wore the eye-mask that had been the free gift of an airline some years previously and which he maintained ensured better sleep. 'Just another dig at me for getting these curtains wrong,' Claire chuckled to herself. She loved James, was used to his ways and she needed his support over the seemingly endless problems with her mother.

She rose quietly and putting on her dressing gown went to the loo before starting downstairs. She took a deep breath before opening the Dining Room door.

Caroline meanwhile had managed to work herself up in preparation of the arrival of her daughter. She raised her bloated, tear-stained face and tried to focus on Claire standing in the doorway gazing impassively back. Caroline had not yet decided whether to be the pitiful object of misery (in which case she knew to expect little) or aggressive – either way this would be a challenging scene between the two women, which motivated one and exhausted the other.

Claire went and filled a glass with water from the tap in the kitchen next door and held it out to her mother. She felt a wave or irritation flow over her and a surge of self-pity at the injustice of having to be the one to feed, clean and house this woman, her mother. The expectation that she would listen to unintelligible justifications of the appalling behaviour, but no gratitude, no affection, nothing but even more demands – this was the basis of their relationship.

Ever since her father's death, seven years previously, Claire had felt compelled to do her best for her surviving parent. For months she had been aware of the need to free herself and James from this situation, but nobody could, or would, take their place. Myra, the eldest, lived abroad, Beattie, the youngest, had several young children and a husband who controlled every penny, Charlie and Archie were both overseas as serving officers in the army.

Claire and James's children were both at university, so it fell to them to sort things out for Caroline.

'Stupid little cow,' said Caroline, having decided on nastiness when confronted with the water. 'Get me a gin and tonic, and make sure I can taste the gin.'

She still lay on the floor with her head propped up against the wall. The smell of urine was over-powering and Claire stepped over her mother to the window and opened it before turning back to confront her mother again.

'OK,' said Claire firmly, 'I'm not giving you anything except water, or maybe a cup of tea if you prefer, so get that clear please.' She stepped back quickly as she saw that her mother was trying to reach her with her legs to deliver a kick. 'You have two choices. The first is that I will help you get up, have a bath, something to eat and then go to see the doctor because (she took another deep breath to reinforce her decision) James and I are not going to carry on like this. Your second choice is that you can stay where you are, lying in your own filth, and I will call Social Services to do something about you because James and I will be leaving to go and have a break away. It's up to you. Which is it to be?'

It was still possible to see that Caroline had been a beautiful girl. Now aged 67 her hair, though thin and fine, had lost none of its rich brown colour, but her brow was permanently furrowed and her nose purple and bulbous, the legacy of years of excessive alcoholic consumption. Her eyes, always behind tinted glasses, consequently appeared larger than they were and there was a look of malevolence compounded by the firmly pursed lips. A small woman with large breasts, she somehow managed to hold herself in a straight-backed posture, when she could hold herself up at all. Overall her aura was one of intimidation and malice. However, to everyone's astonishment, it was still possible to see occasional glimpses of the sunny nature with the sharp fast wit that had attracted so many people, not least the man who had been her husband for over forty years.

This was the face that she had now decided to produce for Claire. She was shocked by the ultimatum and to realise that she was not in a position to demand anything. She started backtracking fast.

Smiling broadly, she looked up at Claire standing implacably by the door, and lifted her arms in a gesture of supplication. 'Oh dear, I seem to have upset you Darling. I really am so sorry.' Making every effort to look contrite she continued 'I'll have that glass of water now.' Whilst drinking she watched her child over the rim of the glass and tried to calculate her next move.

The 'phone rang and Claire's voice softened from her initial 'hello' when she heard her daughter's voice. 'Hello Helen. How are you Darling?'

'Is everything OK Mum, you sound strained?' Helen adored her mother above all others. She was fond of her father too but he couldn't produce the same response in his daughter – that of watchful adoration.

Claire struggled to sound jolly when she said 'Yes, everything's fine.' There was a catch in her voice that didn't dupe Helen who sighed and said:

'It's Granny again I suppose?' There was a silence between the two women. Whilst Helen waited, Claire fought her emotion at the instinctive support given and her desire to protect Helen from the current situation.

Claire let out a long breath, 'Mmm, it's quite difficult just now...' She was interrupted by the pathetic whimpering of her mother who had somehow managed to get to her feet and was holding herself up in the doorway from the hall to the dining room.

'I've got to go Helen. Sorry Darling. I'll ring you later.' She replaced the receiver and moved quickly to her mother just managing to protect her head from injury as she slid once more to the floor.

Claire sat on the floor next to her mother, who was making unintelligible noises, and putting her hands over her face she started to cry.

'That's it. I've had enough of this.' James was standing on the stairs looking down at the scene below. 'I'm ringing for an ambulance.' He lifted Claire to her feet and held her against him for a few seconds before reaching for the 'phone.

Two weeks later and Claire was sitting in her kitchen opposite her sister who had flown in from Spain to see their mother. 'Nothing like another drama to bring her over.' Claire thought.

Myra looked disdainfully around her as a matter of course when she was near Claire. Living as she did in an 18th century nobleman's house just outside Madrid, having married a Spaniard, borne him two children and enjoyed the wealth and position he had bestowed upon her, she found her younger sister's way of life 'dreary and suburban' and didn't try and conceal her distaste. Claire always enjoyed calling her sister 'Contessa' in revenge, knowing how cross that made her.

'Are Charlie and Archie coming today?' Myra asked.

'No, Myra, I've already told you, it's just you and me. The boys are both away and frankly not that interested anyway.' Myra winced and Claire knew it wasn't just because of their brothers.

'I can't do anything either can I? Living abroad and travelling around so much.'

Claire sat with her hands in her lap and looked carefully at her sister for some minutes, watching her become uncomfortable and uneasy under this scrutiny.

'Why are you here then? If you aren't prepared to help, what possible use do you think you are?' Claire continued to gaze steadily, making sure that there was no other expression on her face other than polite enquiry.

'I just want Mummy to know that I care about her and that I support her.' Myra's voice had risen as she tried to defend herself.

'Oh really,' sarcasm had crept into Claire's voice and she felt herself flush with annoyance, 'and how does this 'support' manifest itself? Was that what happened when Charlie, Archie and I had got her safely ensconced in Worthing, with a perfectly nice woman to look after her. We had all the standing orders organised, carpets down, curtains up etc., when you turned up on one of your fleeting visits in a chauffeur-driven limousine and told your mother that you didn't like her flat and that, horror of horrors, you thought the whole building was 'common.' Was that supportive? Is that your idea of helpful?' By this time Claire was furious. The recollection of the episode had reminded her of how little help Myra had ever been, not just in this, but in everything.

'I didn't tell her to leave though did I?' Myra's voice was strident.

'Oh don't be so naïve. Mummy has always been so impressed by your lifestyle, your expensive clothes and money. You were, in her terms, her most successful daughter. She was a wealthy woman but you have achieved all those things that she would have liked for herself – a seriously rich husband, a glittering social life with the famous and infamous, international travel. If you thought something was 'common' she couldn't possibly stay there – certainly not if you said it. Do you remember where we went from there? Probably not. There have been so many moves haven't there? But how could you know anything about the logistics? You never involved yourself did you?' Claire's hostility had forced Myra to her feet and she stood looking out of the window into the garden, taking the blow of her sister's words on her back.

If Claire had been able to see Myra's face, she would have been even more infuriated. For Myra's countenance held a smirk. 'I don't care what you think Mrs Prissy Claire,' thought Myra as she registered the width and breadth of the garden. 'Ye Gods, what a dump this is. I couldn't bring Jose here he would hate it. So suburban.' To Myra's mind this was even more damning than 'common'.

Jose was much older than Myra but when they met his twenty-two years seniority had melted away for them both. Whilst he adored his wife, he was also very strict and veneration for the older generation was paramount to his culture, not least because he was only two years younger than his mother-in-law.

'Are we going to see her or not?' Myra demanded, completely ignoring her sister's rebuke.

'I saw her yesterday. You go' Claire said tiredly. Knowing quite well that Myra despised everything about her, she didn't feel like defending herself, her husband, her home and her opinions just for the sake of keeping up appearances. 'When are you going back to Spain?'

'Oh soon, I think' Myra said breezily. 'I'll spend a couple of days in the London flat and see some friends, so I'll go straight on from the hospital today shall I?'

'Yes' Claire said simply, feeling the relief at her sister's imminent departure wash over her. Neither of them made any pretence at affection or deluded themselves that the other would mind the parting.

After Myra had left Claire went and pulled the sheets off the spare-room bed, threw open the windows and cleaned the guest bathroom. Whilst she did so, she thought about her conversation with the accountant yesterday. 'Oh, bloody hell' she thought resentfully, 'another bloody day wasted on my mother'.

The 'phone rang. It was James. 'How's your day going?' he had a chuckle in his voice. 'Has the ghastly sister-in-law gone yet?'

She smiled; glad that James was there, understanding how difficult her situation was with her mother, how difficult it had always been. Her husband didn't like Claire's family. They had always treated him with disdain; except for her father who gave him the impression that he owed something to his second daughter and was obsequious to the point of being annoying. Of course the name didn't help. Drury wasn't anything special but Brown was positively 'prosaic'.

'Yes, she's just left, and she's going straight to London after visiting Mummy so we won't see her here again for a while, thank God'.

'Any luck with finding a nursing home?' James knew that this was the next task for his over-burdened wife.

'No, I haven't had time yet. The thing is, most of them already know about her and won't have her or she has already been and got thrown out.'

'I know darling' James spoke quietly. 'It's such a dilemma, but I'll help in any way I can – as you know. Hey-ho, I'd better crack on, we're busy today'. James was Finance Director for a local engineering company, a job he loved. He was well paid and well respected and the fact that he lived nearby was an added bonus.

After the call ended Claire held the receiver to her cheek and thought about James. 'He always cheers me up, even when things are this bleak.' She smiled as she thought about him and felt better.

Later that day Claire sent the final email. Confirmation had gone to a new nursing home with a copy to the accountants who were transferring money to secure the place. Her mother's meagre possessions were being transported from their store the following day in time for her to arrive by ambulance during the next afternoon and the hospital had been informed as to where her mother was going and the time that the private ambulance would arrive to collect her. There was just one more call to make.

'Peter? This is Claire.' There was silence at the end of the line. 'Claire Brown. Actually I'm your niece.' She felt the surge of dislike she always experienced when she talked to him. But she had to talk to him since he was the only remaining member of her mother's family left alive and he seemed to take an interest in his sister's welfare.

'Oh yes. Hello Claire. How are you?' He replied.

Unprepared to chat or exchange niceties with him Claire said 'I thought I'd let you know where Mummy is going. She's leaving the hospital tomorrow and they've agreed to take her at the St. Nicholas Nursing Home in Stanton, near you. She hasn't been to this one before, but I gather it's very nice and she can afford it.'

'Why doesn't your rich-bitch sister put up some cash to pay for the best?' Peter's dismissal from the bosom of his sister's family still rankled and he'd never forgiven Myra for telling her tales. He'd continued to care for Caroline and even though he'd had multiple problems with wives and children he kept as near to her as he could.

'So, she'll be there about 4pm if you wanted to go and see her. She's got a telephone going in but I don't have the number yet. Alright?' Claire didn't acknowledge that she'd heard what he'd said. She'd conveyed what she wanted to say and she certainly wasn't going to indulge her uncle by discussing anything but the business at hand.

The conversation finished. 'I'm going to have a drink' Claire said out loud. 'I don't care if it is only 5 o'clock. When I've finished that one' she continued dramatically' I'm going to have another one and possibly one after that'. She didn't realise that she'd been heard and was startled then amused when she heard James's voice behind her saying, 'Jolly good idea. I'll do the same' before he wrapped his arms around her and tucked her head under his chin.

Moon Baby

Nobody asked if I wanted to be
I suppose someone discussed it – nobody asked me.
So my soul was selected from the celestial shelf
I was told I was female with wonderful health
Had I known what was coming – the plans down the line
I might have resisted - demanded more time.

Of course we're not told how many we'll do
I had hoped for seven – 'they' might stop me at two
And since not every entity is given the chance
Of this reincarnation, this sweet happenstance
To revisit the earth or other living stars
I must try to enjoy it – I hope it's not Mars.

So, the Moonscape it is – not cheesy at all
Nor green or blue, there's no change in the fall.
It's dusty and drab, just like they told us
And covered with lots of foreign detritus
With one tattered flag on the other side
Which we access by hitching a solar ride.

My new home's quite different and nobody breathes
There's no rain and no wind to rustle the leaves
We don't eat –we don't need water or food

We've no hair or teeth, no organs, no blood
A small clock is placed in our centre to start
To wind down slowly, in place of a heart.

My group is eclectic and there's only one youngster
And it's me, I grow on, the colour of tungsten.
My task is quite simple - I monitor Earth
I love seeing the excitement, equipment, the dearth
Of ideas they might have to try and see us
Looking only at our bad side, covered in dust!

Patrick's Interview

Father Francis O'Brien led Patrick Broughton into his study. As Patrick looked around the familiar room he appreciated the signs of diligence to the Catholic faith. There was the portrait of the holy mother over the mantelpiece, the piles of books and manuscripts and the musty smell of dust, incense and overcooked cabbage that many priests seemed to attract and take with them on their clothing.

'What can I do for you Patrick? Are the family all well?' The priest noted the signs of strain on his visitor's face and the tension showing now in the movement of his fingers. He smiled encouragingly.

'Yes, thank you Father. Everyone's very well and Mary seems to be settling nicely in London. She's sharing a flat with Anne Bewley – it's nice to think of the two of them setting out together.' Patrick gabbled out the words, suddenly overwhelmed by acute embarrassment. He'd practised his words several times in the bathroom and in the car, but now confronted by his spiritual adviser with his gentle manner and wise ways, all he could think was that he wanted to burst into tears.

'And how's your lovely wife?' the Priest probed.

'Yes, she's very well' Patrick took a gulp of air. 'Actually I've come to see you about her – well about our marriage really. Things are difficult.' The wretched man coloured deeply and felt sweat beads appear on his brow.

Used to dealing with problems, and aware that he'd only got half an hour before taking confession, the Priest decided to take a gamble. 'Things in the bedroom OK are they? You know Patrick that sex is a divine gift between man and wife as well, of course, as the children that follow for the blessed ones.'

Patrick blurted out 'I've tried everything but Veronica won't do as I ask any more. She doesn't even join us for prayers and, although she completes her daily tasks as usual, she seems distant.' He glanced at the Priest who saw the anger in his visitor's eyes. 'She deliberately ignores me if I tell her to do something.'

'And the bedroom?' insisted the Priest.

'Well, we had to give all that up after Rachel was born. The doctor told me that any further children would endanger Veronica's life and I couldn't have that could I? I couldn't be left to look after four children on my own.'

'So there's no physical contact between the two of you and Rachel is how old now?' Francis O'Brien sighed worriedly.

'She's just coming up for thirteen' Patrick stammered, suddenly horribly aware that he might be being criticised.

'You've clearly been very silly Patrick Broughton' the Priest could not control his facial expression. There was clear dismay that a man of Patrick's intelligence, the one he'd always praised as being a model husband and father, could be such a fool. 'How can you expect to maintain a happy marriage if you don't show love to your wife? Do you show your affection in any other form?'

'Of course. I provide for them all and I make sure that I know what everyone is up to.' Patrick had resumed his usual pompous self-assuredness.

'And that's it, is it?' Father O'Brien sat back in his seat. 'She's a woman for God's sake man. You have obviously been treating her just as a house-keeper but, just like everybody else, she has needs.'

Patrick thought the words but never said 'What do you know about physical relationships with women?' He felt petulant and a sullen expression settled over his features. He stared at the desk in front of him and waited for the other man to speak again.

The Priest rose. 'Well, it seems to me that you must have had a very unhappy wife and she's obviously done very well in spite of it. I recommend that you take a sexual interest in Veronica again – try and get back into bed together. Do you need advice on anything?'

Patrick assumed, shaking his head, that contraception was being discussed, although neither of them could, of course, utter the word.

'We'll pray together Patrick' said Father O'Brien kneeling down at the small altar against the wall and waited for the other man to join him.

(excerpt from A Middle Aged Love Story)

The New Car

My old man needs a new car
He's identified one, that's not too far
From our house, our budget and useful size
So it seems I must join him to help devise
His strategy for a ridiculous low cost
An area where I am totally lost
For what do I know about engines and things?
I just turn the key and hope the thing sings.

So. Here we are with this earnest young man
Who is keen to show us all that he can
Of the inside and outside and underside yet
Notwithstanding the contents under the bonn-et.
Both men are excited, the talking gets quicker
I worry briefly about my husband's ticker.
He says "wonderful features – are you aware?"
I smile but, honestly, I don't really care.

At last he reluctantly lets got of the wheel
And I am released from this casing of steel.
The sweaty young man says "Well, what do you say?"
My husband asks what's his best deal today?
My opinion's not sought. It does not matter
So I turn my attention to what's for supper.

After all, this episode's only for a car
And without proper food, we won't get far!

A Little Christmas Story

Polly listened carefully as her Father read her the story of Baby Jesus. She nodded at him encouragingly when he appeared to have finished.

'Well then, Daddy. Did he or didn't he turn into a handsome prince?'

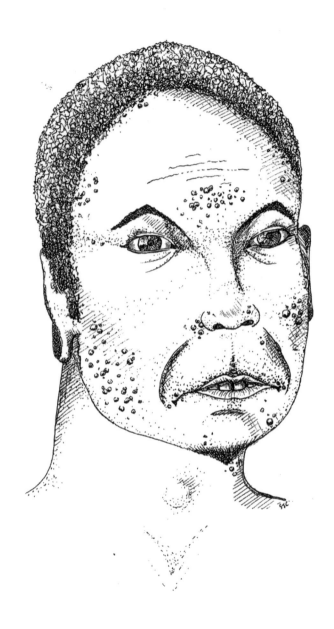

Bad Blood

Oh how I loathe the blood that courses through my veins
Reflecting my long-held wish that I had been born to
    other parents
In another time maybe, another place, another coloured
    skin
Or even not at all, anything rather than this position
    amidst those who try to vilify me and persuade others
    that I am NOT as I really am.

Genetically I'm a muddle. There's some strong evidence
    of oriental -
But not granted me are the loveliest haze of greens or
    deep brown eyes.
More alike are mine to the golden ones of a lion with
    tiny pupils. Dangerous.
Neither do I have the thick strong black hair I crave
Mine is thin with fuzz around my forehead indicating
    some Black African intrusion with a huge bald spot at
    the back.
My lips are thin, my nose too small and my 'Adams
    apple' bobs constantly whatever I do with my throat.

But wait man. I must wait.

Because outside this unhappy frame of humanity there is
more than me.

I must, I must and I must look outwards until my time is
done.

And – I will, because I can and I should and reward will
come.

Elderly Calm

By the time you have elderly calm, you have earned it!
Oh wonderful feeling of inability to change something
And no more the desire to legislate, manipulate, calculate
Alter or direct situations where your voice is no longer
    heard
Because you are old now and, after all, what do you
    know?
How soothing to sit back and watch tensions rise
    knowing
That it is all completely unnecessary, often futile and bad
    for you!
When you have achieved elderly calm you will recognise
    it in others
But the animals know at once and even the wildest
    puppy will quieten at your side
And small children will settle on your shoulder.

You cannot teach anyone how to have elderly calm, all
    you can do is
Point out to them the wisdom of your ways and the error
    of theirs!
It helps if you lower your voice to its deepest point and
    talk slowly

People tend to listen if you do that – nobody likes the
  idea of being
Perceived to be deaf! This takes the sting out of ire!
Perhaps this is why older people often lose their vocal
  strength.
Elderly calm requires that you say little anyway and
  therefore
The sipping of tea, wine, gin or water becomes even
  more pleasurable.

Oh happy days when you can look deep into the heart of
  a flower,
And rub your fingers over a leaf to find the veins that
  bring it life.
To listen to the breeze working its way through all
  matter even the
limp deadness of fallen debris from the canopy above.
To watch the frantic scurry of small insects as they gather
  in for their short lives
And to smile as the first rays of sunshine layer across the
  grass as they
Appear from clouds spinning high above.
To reflect on all the colours – from the deep azure of a
  thunderous sky
As it drifts towards you over rape, wheat, linseed and
  barley -
And always the greens. The magic of May, the smell of
  mown grass,
The bittersweet smell of newly turned earth
The taste of that first tomato that has been nurtured and
  the tang of
The cox's orange pippin that you caught before it fell.

The roses and clematis and all those other old friends
that have appeared
To cheer you, year after year, and the annuals with their
temporariness.
And of course the birds, which become friends as they
see you more
And then sing sweet and clear from next door's chimney
all summer long.
Autumn and Winter flow smoothly towards you, each
with their
Gifts of light and colour, sights and sounds.
All these things and so much more are yours when you
have elderly calm.

So – when it is your turn to die, there is no real tragedy
because
With elderly calm you know that you will return to the
heart of matters and
That your voice will be carried on the wind and your face
reflected in a flower
For those that loved you enough to find you. In streams
and puddles, waves and
Lakes, high or low, inside or out, warm or cold, loud or
quiet, there you will be
Until there is no-one left to remember you or your
elderly calm!

But that's right isn't it? It's a triumph. All is well.

The Postcard

I've just found this. Eleanor, my only daughter, sent it to me along with the other photographs she took on their honeymoon – just one year ago. Guy had decided against a foreign trip because he said he wanted to introduce his new wife to sailing and he was familiar with these waters in Dorset. As always, Eleanor had complied with his wishes.

The wedding had been the best day of my life. Both her father and I had marvelled at Eleanor's serenity after her exhausting medical finals. We were both so proud of our petite daughter with her waist-length hair piled up on her head, held there by the family coronet and her full-length veil. I cried with happiness that day because I allowed myself to accept that Eleanor was right and I was wrong in thinking that Guy wasn't good enough for her. Seeing her so happy, I had felt ashamed to have questioned her choice.

I'm trying to decide whether or not to send the picture to Guy with a note. But what can I write? What can I say to him that won't exacerbate my rage and bitterness? I don't want to write to him or talk to him or hear his name – I simply want to murder him, because he killed Eleanor.

On the back of the picture Eleanor had written 'Now my most favourite place in the world!' Later she told me that she and Guy had sat on chairs like this, under this very tree – shaded from the sun at the end of a day on the water. They had sat nursing cold Chablis and savouring the expectation of a wonderful dinner. During the following weeks my Eleanor told me that she had never been this happy. She bubbled over with it – her eyes shone and she sang constantly until – suddenly – she went quiet.

I look at the picture and climb into it. What must it have been like to be the gardener who found the empty bottles of pills and whisky and the single envelope, addressed to her father and me? She had placed the items carefully on one chair and laid her wedding dress neatly on the other.

What must my child have endured before she tottered to the water's edge? Guy killed her with his betrayal and his announcement, ten months after their wedding, that he had made a bad mistake and that he was leaving her for someone else.

After some time, I conclude that this is a picture of Eleanor's greatest happiness and endless sorrow. I have decided to keep it.

Toddler – Getting Me Off To Sleep

'It's time for you to go to sleep
I don't want to hear another peep
Hush now, stop it. Be a good lad.
Now come on sweetheart, don't make me mad.'

'You've had your story and been to the loo
Cleaned your teeth and you're tired out too
One more cuddle, a kiss and a hug
Then you must settle down like a bug in a rug.'

My darling Mummy has left me alone
I've tried everything and now I lie prone
I'm pounding my teddy and kicking the bed
I'm feeling so cross and have turned a dark red

Ah good, my Dad's home and has entered my room
I'll continue to scream –an impressive volume
'Come on young man that's quite enough
You sometimes do make life quite tough.'

He's raised his voice. I think he means business
I hold up my arms and await words of kindness
'It's the end of the day, Mum and I are tired too

Settle down now my son. God bless you.'

I can hear them talking, but not what they say
I can hear cupboards opening, plates put away
I can hear music playing and the hum of the heating
What, I wonder.... Can...
                              ... they
                                    be ......

The Quiet Ones

Please don't think that because I'm quiet and say little
That I have no opinion. I just don't like tattle-tittle
Don't assume I know nothing because I choose not to say
What I think of the latest gossip that day.

Don't imagine I'm a no-one with no qualifications
For all you know I'm clever enough to run a power
    station.
Perhaps you believe that this soft little lady
Has no other use than to cook and clean daily.

And what does that mean, you ignorant oaf?
That my life is well spent watching a loaf
Rise in a bowl with damp clothe atop it
Or hoovering for England awaiting your visit.

Whilst you spout your views to anyone who'll listen
Mine is a more modest approach and I must hasten
To add that I find you worryingly ignorant
With views more appropriate to an uneducated peasant.

Naturally I can say nothing of this because of my
    breeding
But as the door closes behind you, when you're finally
    leaving

I can slip into my bathroom and give vent to my desire
To call you all the names I know: Bastard, Fool and Liar.

The Longest Kiss

The longest kiss started soon after we met
With almost no meeting of our waiting lips
And continued like the whisper of a summer breeze
Across the ripening wheat on the farmland by my home.

Of course life intervened and we had a past to vanquish
Though time and courage did their work at last
Once passion was assuaged and sexual panic soothed
There came reassurance that the other would be there.

Thereafter every night and day, some part of us would
    touch
To show the kiss was still in view waiting for the time
To touch the other, soft lips on cheek or lips or hair
'I love you' it says and so much better than any words.

Different Sickness

I notice your reactions when you see her there
You try to smile brightly. You try not to stare
How should you face her, and what can you say?
When you know how she struggles each moment - each
    day?

You want to think kindly and give her of your best
But her misery appals you and who could have guessed
That, even with money, good looks, a fine home
She would end up so ill, so frightened, so alone?

The words out, I know, that she's been in a clinic
So that soft-spoken psychos cured her with their magic
After all their education, seminars and stuff
Which had no effect at all on her - what a lot of guff.

This is an illness unlike any other
Therefore it's harder and takes longer to recover
Please smile when you see her, help her get well
Don't exacerbate this endless and ghastly living hell.

Flab

I sometimes look back to when I was a girl
With a trim little figure and head full of curls
Blonde hair that was natural; I liked being me
When my bra size was tiny – now 36D

The mini-skirts then were a sight to behold
They just hid my knickers but I felt no cold
With the warmth of the gaze of the men I passed by
Or was it my boots that went right up my thigh?

I mothered three children like many girls do
Nursing them carefully and watching them chew
At my sweet little bosoms which after a while
Became flaccid and heavy, a nuisance, a trial.

Over the years I have fought with the loss
Of elasticity, glamour and gloss
I have rubbed creams, oils and potions all over the place
With particular emphasis now on my face.

When showered and rubbed dry I look with self-pity
At those areas responding to forces of gravity
But, in my mind's eye, I am still that young thing
Pretty and laughing, just gorgeous and thin!

Found Out

It is the early hours of the morning. The door into an expensively decorated flat opens and the light flicks on. There is the aroma of expensive perfume often used, and a faint scent of French cigarettes. A woman enters. She is crying. She leaves the door open and we can hear other footsteps approach. She turns as Jamie enters the room.

Jamie: You can't keep on grieving like this Annie.

Annie: I can. I could cry forever.
You shouldn't have hit him. I didn't want you to hit him.

Jamie: Maybe not, but I wanted to hit him. Actually I wanted to kill him.

Annie: I knew something was going on. I've suspected for months but, until tonight, I had no proof.

She sat down suddenly on the arm of a sofa.

Annie: I'm going to leave him. I have no choice. My God, he's going to pay for this.

Jamie: They were planning a little 'love nest' in, of all places, Basingstoke. [He *sniggered*]. I find it all quite funny. I'm furious of course, but I can see the amusing side too.

Annie: It's <u>not</u> funny. I have four young children and we have all been let down [*more tears*].

Jamie: Have you got anything to drink?

Annie: Yes, I'm so sorry Jamie. What would you like?

Jamie: Whisky please. [*pause whilst he collects the glass and sits down*].
Have you always been a faithful wife? You can tell me to mind my own bloody business but I probably wouldn't have the nerve to ask you another time!

Annie: It's OK. You've been very kind, especially this evening. Technically, I have been faithful. I haven't actually been to bed with anyone else since we got married, but I suppose I've flirted quite outrageously and led people on sometimes.

Jamie: [*Watching her carefully over the rim of his glass*] Yes, I'm the same, but I don't think you and I have flirted with each other, have we?

Annie: [*with a laugh*] No, we have been too busy watching your wife and my husband!

Jamie: Nice to see you smile! You will get over this and so will I. I have no intention of staying with Barbara. She's done this before and I've had enough.
Might I have another drink?

[Annie pours another large one for them both]

Annie: I shall never forget the expression on their faces when we walked in. They looked so silly didn't they? I was pleased to see Barbara looks quite fat and flabby with no clothes on and those great tombstone teeth! Ed's face was a picture. Did you notice that he had kept his socks on?

[Laughter]

James: I suppose Ed forgot you had a key to the business flat had he? Or did he never think that you suspected him and would burst in?

Annie: Both probably. I always use this place when I come to London. It belongs to me. Dolphin Court belongs to the business. It doesn't matter because there's no going back now.
          What will you do Jamie? Maybe it's easier for you because you have no children.

Jamie: Must be true. I don't know yet. I might go and live in France. She's got her own money so Barbara can have the house, but that's all and I will have enough to get a little place, keep a boat, play golf and eat well. Actually, it all sounds lovely. *[He laughs]*

Annie: It does. I may have to come and visit you.

Jamie: Let's have another drink.

[They sit quietly and sip their drinks. Then Annie starts to cry softly]

Jamie: Oh dear, poor little thing. Come here and let
           me give you a hug.

[*He hugs her and she buries her face in his chest, weeping quietly.
He lifts her face to his and kisses her tenderly on the lips*.........]

The Tale Of Bo Walters

Bo Walters, gardener, is in his mid-thirties, unkempt and completely indifferent to hygiene. He generally has enough dirt under his fingernails to grow seeds. He's worn the same clothes for years and replaces anything he needs from the irregular jumble sales held in the village hall.

An amiable character, simple but straightforward he loves most animals, especially dogs, but he doesn't like cats – especially the one living at his place of work which is the garden attached to the biggest house in the village.

Bo's dislike for felines stemmed from the time when he had received a beating from his father when he was ten years old, for allegedly taking some cold chicken which had been left on the kitchen table at home. He knew quite well that the family cat, a flea-bitten old tom called Max, had been the culprit. In spite of all his protests of innocence the boy had watched his father remove his old leather belt and swish it through the air before landing it on his son's bent posterior several times. When the punishment was over Bo straightened and turned his anguished face to his mother for comfort. But she was cuddling the traitorous Max, making sure that he wasn't distressed by the violence of the scene. Bo made eye contact with Max who gazing back and blinking slowly conveyed the correct impression of satisfaction. Bo never forgot the beating or forgave the cat.

This strange man helps himself to food from the woods and once a week visits the village store for his other groceries. He quite enjoys meeting people outside the shop and often engages in long conversations, apparently unaware of rain, snow, heat or cold. The tolerant population takes it in turns to endure the half-hour usually required to persuade Bo that it's time to go.

Everyone in the small community knows Bo and after his family had all perished in a house fire when he was sixteen, there has been a collective awareness of his vulnerability. His name is often on the vicar's list for the pastoral committee and the general consensus is that Bo isn't a source of danger to anyone and that he's generally comfortable and content.

Home is a caravan that his employers have allowed him to place in the woods at the furthest point from the mansion and near some derelict buildings formerly used by the family when they organised shooting parties. He was able to buy the caravan when Mrs Willis, appalled by Bo's situation, organised an appeal in the village. There was enough money to buy the second-hand home and enough too for a bicycle with a little left in the bank for emergencies.

The woods are, Bo has always felt sure, there specifically for him. He loves the contours and the shadows, the leaning trees and the large craters – a legacy from the last war when the German's dropped their excess bombs after a raid on Cardiff. He smells the same as the earth which he lifts and sniffs every day of his life. He smiles as he kneels, especially when in a swathe of bluebells and watches the patches of light move across them as the tree canopy yields to the breeze and lets the sunlight through.

Rubbing a handful of wet leaves over his face causes him to laugh out loud, exultant with joy at his fulfilment. He feels cleansed when he does this and it's his only method of ablution. Unsurprisingly, Bo has very few teeth left in his head and the loss of each one has been greeted with surprised interest.

The creatures who share the wood with Bo are used to his presence and he once befriended a dog fox that he'd rescued and taken to his caravan when the hunters had driven the animal, exhausted and terrified, into the sheds nearby.

'No I 'aint seen no fox,' he lied, when the group of riders and their dogs came by. The dogs were howling around the caravan but Bo stood his ground and eventually the party moved on. John Willis, his employer's youngest son, grinned at Bo from astride his huge mount. John had respect for this strange man who refused to comply with the constraints of modern living. He was almost certain that Bo knew where the fox was but he didn't consider insulting him by asking for a look inside his home.

Bo has worked for the Willis family ever since he left school at sixteen and shortly after he was orphaned. He hadn't enjoyed his school life – the strictures of the classroom made him feel uncomfortable and cross and he longed for the hours to pass so that he could get back to the woods. He had made a camp there and this was where he was, whittling away at a stick, when his family perished after a chip pan caught fire.

Mrs Willis's charity continued and, whether he knew it or not, Bo's welfare was discreetly monitored. He always felt happy. There was nothing that upset or bothered him – except for Mrs Willis's cat – the dreaded Jasper.

Jasper had arrived as a kitten five years ago and it wasn't long before Bo made his feelings known not only to the creature but anyone else who would listen – except of course, Mrs Willis herself whose doting concern for her pet denied her any insight into her gardener's antipathy. On the contrary, she was certain that her beloved cat and the strange man who worked in her garden had a huge bond. She had noticed and been warmed by how much time they seemed to spend together.

For the cat's part and with a haughty style to his movement, Jasper would make a point of approaching Bo in whatever part of the garden he was working. He would often sit and make himself comfortable just far enough away from Bo to avoid being disturbed but near enough to enjoy staring maliciously at his prey. Jasper had a white marking by his mouth which made him look, Mrs Willis said, as though he was always smiling. 'Little Darling' she called him. Bo didn't dare chase the little animal for fear of being seen by Mrs Willis who would sometimes be carrying her cat when she came to discuss the gardening. The cat would sit in the confines of Mrs Willis's ample bosom and, although he tried not to look, there was, Bo felt a definite air of superiority about the creature, a smirk, which antagonised him even more.

One Thursday morning in June, Bo was enjoying feeling the hot sunshine on his back as he knelt over his task of weeding the large rose bed situated in the middle of the circular drive. In the centre of the flower bed a marble statue of a woman stands with her arms raised in supplication. Bo had already cleared the area around the plinth, trimmed the edges and he was removing individual weeds with the careful use of a small fork. As he worked Bo loosened the soil and softly sang the only song he knew – the first verse of the hymn, 'Dear Lord and Father of Mankind.'

Suddenly, the cat dashed from the other side of the statue and started vigorously scratching at the patch of earth that Bo had just completed. To his fury, Bo realised that the cat was preparing a toilet.

'Getoff you bugger,' growled Bo, but the cat, indulged and confident, turned its back and squatted over the hole it had just made about a foot from Bo's outstretched arm. It heaved and quivered as it discharged excrement into the hole. The wonderful smell of early roses, the fresh air and newly turned earth were overpowered by the noxious fumes emitting from the cat.

Bo, enraged, lifted his fork and struck the cat on the head. A long trickle of blood appeared from the wound as the cat fell to the side and with glazed eyes ceased to breathe.

For a long moment Bo didn't move. He was trying to absorb what had happened. Looking at the house to see if he'd been seen, Bo grabbed the small corpse, appalled at what he'd done and terrified of the consequences, he continued to dig feverishly about in the earth with one hand whilst forcing the dead cat up his pullover with the other.

He started to mutter. 'Oh lawks, what's going to happen now? Mrs Willis will be so upset. I might lose my job and then what'll happen to me?' As he carried on with his task, the enormity of his crime hit him and large tears started to roll down his face leaving vertical tracks on his grimy cheeks.

After a little while when his heart beat had returned to normal Bo stood up. With his back to the house and the cat still tucked up inside his clothing, he strolled casually to the end of the garden where he couldn't be seen and dropped the corpse over the hedge meaning to return later to bury it.

Bo had a wretched day after that. Mrs Willis and her friend, Mrs Phillimore, returned to the house at lunchtime and made a point of viewing the rose bed and talking to Bo. He could hardly look at his benefactress but she noticed the water marks on his cheeks and frowned with a tinge of worry that he might have been upset.

'Is everything all right Bo?' she asked, but he just nodded and carried on with his work.

The woods that night were eerily still as Bo crept in the moonlight to locate the dead animal. There was no sign. He moved up and down with his pencil torch but he couldn't find it. Shrugging he muttered to himself, 'Daresay the old fox has it.' Feeling satisfied that he had done his best he went home.

The next morning was another lovely day and Bo felt optimistic and happy. After all, his tormentor had gone and no-one had accused him of anything. He gathered up his tools to start work and was just leaving the shed when Mrs Willis appeared. She was agitated and upset. Bo could see that she had been crying and he felt sorry. He liked her and she had always been kind to him.

'Oh Bo,' said Mrs Willis, fighting to control her emotion. 'I'm afraid I have such bad news and I know that you'll be upset too. We've lost our little cat, Jasper. He didn't come in for his supper and eventually John found him down there.' She pointed towards the hedge. 'We think he must have been hit by a car and just crept off to die – they do that you know.' Unable to fight it any longer, Mrs Willis broke down and wept.

Bo had never felt so miserable in his life. He moved his weight from foot to foot and Mrs Willis, looking at him, said. 'Oh I'm sorry Bo. How selfish of me. I know how fond of Jasper you were. You must be very sad too.' Somewhat relieved, Bo managed to nod.

'Right then,' said Mrs Willis after sniffing delicately and dabbing her nose with a lacy handkerchief, 'would you please dig a grave for Jasper and then we can have a little ceremony. I thought it would be appropriate for him to go in the rose bed at the front – you know, under the statue where you were working yesterday. That way we will all have a memorial to him.'

Colours In The Sky

The most subtle colours ever designed
Are changing each day and I can find
Rich hues of loveliness high in the sky
Waiting to comfort me after I die.

The bare-boned trees of winter, with cold frosty days
Present palest of blues, pinks, yellow and greys.
Then spring's breathtaking blues with a varying shroud
of rolling and threatening rain-filled white cloud.

The fields show their crops now - the richest of greens
On land bask in sunshine, untroubled it seems
Save for indigo violet heralding a storm
But what trouble's expected? How will it form?

Deep waves of black cut through with sunbeam
Misting to oblivion as the rain comes to clean
And refresh summer sky before wind stern and strong
Returns the heavens to where they belong.

And sunsets now blaze with red of every hue
with yellows and pinks, pale lilac – orange too
Whilst over the sea where no man has been
There's that last splash of colour, the striking of green.

But – the deep velvet darkness of a clear autumn night
With the galaxies blazing and the soft moonlight
Are the softest and safest and clearest of all
Show your breath in the stillness and hear the owl call.

Golf

The ladies are in from their round
And the changing room's full of the sound
Of the 'How did you do's?' and 'I'm just giving up'
With the winner who's yet to be found
Out!

'God, look at her thong' whispers one to her friend
'I know' the reply 'she's just trying to pretend
that she's still slim enough to keep trying
to compete with the young and keeps buying
rubbish'!

The queue for the three showers is short
But there's time to indulge in the sport
Of having a look at everyone's things
Oh no, Vanessa has started to sing
Again!

The scent of the sprays fills the air
Since some women have the idea
That hair which is rigid if not actually solid
Might compete with the icon called Olive.
Possibly!

Faces stretched by jewelled fingers apply

Make-up first to the skin then each eye
With a critical look and a smoothing of hips
Tongues run over the teeth and under red lips
In case!

Bags are stuffed with the discarded clothing
Two ladies stare at each other with loathing
Both are wearing the same dark green blazer
'Bet hers comes from Marks. Mine's from Jaegar'
they both think!

Lady Captain enters, flushed and unsteady
'Come on Ladies, are you nearly ready?'
The Chardonnay's showing, She's been in for a while
She knows it and gives a strained smile
Whoops!

I smiled at my partner at lunch
I had already told her my hunch
We'd have chicken parcels in very small sizes
But hang on, they're ready to give out the prizes
Coo!

We sit there politely applauding those
Whose names are called and at the close
Feel sure we could do better with slower greens
And no noise from the groundsmen on their big
    machines
Etc.

The main thing that we must not forget
Is how lucky we are, how fortunate
That we can be in the heavenly country
Playing our game, laughing, harmless and free.

Local Town

Today I went to my local town
Tho' the buildings are fine it's very run down
There's no cathedral, so it's not a city
It's a shambles – a mess, just such a pity.

Walking the main street, I looked at the people
Set against the backdrop of All Saints Church steeple
Mostly they spoke in a language not English
Orientals, Bulgarians, Romanians and Polish

In the middle of the day, why weren't they working?
Some were chatting, others leaning or casually lurking
I wondered if they've come for our benefits system
Which means they do nothing and we look after them.

In several small corners men cross-legged were sitting
Gum-chewing or something and occasionally spitting
Their clothing was different; it looked shabby and worn
And the coats, which they need here, were ancient and
    torn.

Like most native dwellers I'm happy to share
With those who need a new start under our care
But….. they must speak English, acknowledge our laws
Get a job, pay their way, not become a new 'cause'

I feel grief for my country and my grandchildren small
Are we leaving them anything worth having at all?
I'm an ordinary and nice person, glad to be kind
And will probably be penalised for speaking my mind.

In The Café

The trousers are expertly positioned in a rigid line straight across the centre of a stout stomach. They are brown. The green shirt is tucked carefully in with no excess cotton to cause a crease. He is self-assured with his square area of beard carefully positioned underneath the bottom of his first chin and little piggy eyes dart backwards and forwards across the cafeteria.

He's standing in the aisle and the table for four next to him already has two occupants sitting next to the window overlooking the port.

'Vera' he suddenly bellows 'over 'ere. I'm over 'ere' accompanied with a vigorous waving of his free hand. The other is holding his tray lightly on the edge of the table.

The couple next to him jumps visibly and turn to see who and where Vera was.

Inevitably Vera turns out to be even larger than her husband. She's managed to squeeze her large hips into a pair of white cut-off trousers and her tee-shirt, the favourite one disporting shiny monkeys is stuffed optimistically into the waistband.

'Where's Marje?' the husband continues his unabated roaring tone as his wife approaches.

'I think they're just coming in' she counters.

Everyone around is now aware of the quartet's attempt to sit together and a woman sitting on her own, three tables down, a look of supreme irritation on her face, rises slowly, wipes her lips and throwing her napkin onto the debris of breakfast calls out.

'Oh please, do all come and sit here. I'm just going'.

A Winter Night

The sky is full of undelivered snow
To shorten the lives of lambs so white
Harsh winds rush past laden with flakes to go
Across my window turning day to early night.

Outside I hear the silence start to grow
My curtains pulled - my shawl around me tight.
I will withstand this winter's eve alone
There is no power, no fuel, no 'phone.

Later a whistle in the rafters is an isolating sound
I think of those explorers who head off to the Pole
A lonely trek in unimaginable cold surround
Where shelter, like mine, would offer some control.

Fast comes the dawn, once it's decided
To turn on the light and start another day
I gaze with awe at virgin snow in drifts divided
By tops of fence. I have no choice. I'll stay.

Newspaper

When I pick up a paper to read these days
I could throw it across the room
So great is my rage at some issues they raise
And the hurt and the hate and the gloom

Where is the decency, loyalty, honour
Traditional values between one and another?
You can't cuddle a child without being accused
Tenderness these days means 'being abused'

I read recently of a wedding in Troon
Where the bride threw an ashtray at her furious groom
She got drunk, lost her temper and erupted in fury
And ended up single in front of a jury.

Many modern issues concern Arabs and Jews
Who can't bear each other and never eschew
The chance to start battle, cause mayhem, behead
Frightened captives, even women – dreadful bloodshed.

The Tsunami in Thailand, endless war in Iraq
Families separated by service, waiting for young to get
    back
Shootings in revenge for some unwarranted deed

Northern Ireland goes through motions but nothing is
    agreed.

The page three girls still pose with lips slightly apart
Flesh exposed, thrusting forward, and hoping for a start
In the world of show business where ultimate
    degradation
Awaits the unsuccessful – pornography - humiliation.

The politicians are there of course for daily public
    inspection
Of policies, and manoeuvrings before the next election.
I don't believe it's possible now for government to be fair
In spite of the work of Blunkett, Clarke and Mr Tony
    Blair.

The young it would seem are quite out of control
Drinking hugely, shouting loudly and seem on the whole
To be certain the world owes them at least a good living
Without effort on their part, just taking – no giving.

Rich old women give birth to a child manufactured
Outside, in a glass dish, whilst the world's infrastructure
Can't cope with it all and so babies lie helpless
And food is destroyed here because of the excess.

Editorials and letters reflect these modern times
There's no longer any need to try and read between the
    lines
There's no gentleness, no kindness now, just endless
    mortal sin
I think I won't bother any more – I'll put it in the bin.

Hang on, what about the sports page, the crossword and
    the weather

I ought to look at cricket scores after the team's entire
    endeavour
Oh jolly good, we've won the test and we're ready for six
    nations
The cartoon's funny, the forecast's good. I'm rewarded
    for my patience.

The Chair

I am a chair. My deep red leather folds down my long back and across my great wings. My arms curl over in welcome either side of my thickly padded seat and the brass studs that adorn my seams gleam and reflect each particle of light.

I have been placed, quite rightly, with my back to the curve in the wall. From here I can see past my compatriots to the Reception Desk at this most exclusive golf club. My three fellow citizens, also in deep scarlet, do not have a voice – except to convey their thoughts and words to me. It is therefore imperative that I stay where I am so that I can keep control.

Being so heavy, the cleaner hasn't the strength to move me and I heard her being told not to knock our legs with her vacuum but to use a soft brush to remove any dust. Splendid!

On the whole, we feel really good. Everyone seems to like us and we are happy with out situation.

The ladies are interesting. There's one group who clearly want to laugh and enjoy life whilst others seem to flourish on drama and illness, stories of hardship and criticism. One such group of ladies halted close to our 'shrine'.

'I'm going to call that area The Departure Lounge' said one. I felt my skin tighten.

'Well I've never seen chairs like that in any airport' responded one of her friends.

'No, not that sort of departure lounge – I mean' said the first, and she lowered her voice to a whisper whilst rolling her eyes, 'these are the sort of chairs you get in an old people's home'.

All four of us reacted and, if there hadn't been so much nonsensical laughter, the ladies would have heard the the groan of oak and the creak of leather.

'They remind me of those chairs you get in a Gentleman's Club' said another woman. 'You know – those ones where men think they can hide'!

One of the ladies cast an agonised glance in our direction. Did she realise perhaps that we are not as we seem?

And now, suddenly and surprisingly, I find to my great joy that I have a writer. Now I can reveal all the secrets that leak out in this hallowed circle. Is it her? Is it the woman with the wise green eyes who reacted to the offensive abuse? I may never know.

The elderly men like to come and sit on us. I always get the noisier dominant one – presumably because he can hold forth without any interruption from behind! But, my goodness, they do tell fibs.

'I scored a net 73 today' said one, but I knew he was lying. I could feel it through the tightness of his stomach as he pulled it in towards his back. His head leant against my back and I read his brain. 'I'm sure nobody saw me move my ball in the rough'.

A beautiful girl came and perched down. She was as light as a feather and barely made an impact on my seat as her weight, such as it was, balanced on the wooden frame. It was an interview and I could feel her tremble slightly and a fragile mist floated around her as her apprehension increased. It all went well and the short young man wearing his only expensive suit gave her his assurance that employment was imminent.

The small numbers of children always visit us, attracted no doubt by our lovely colour and the brass 'smarties'. We like to feel their energetic little limbs and small fingers prying and poking down the deep recesses of our seats.

Oh hello, it's the woman with the wise green eyes here again. She smiles as she walks towards me, comes up behind me and rests her hands at the top of my broad being. She squeezes me gently and bends to rub her face gently across the softness of my skin.

'I know you' she said quietly. Her voice was as soft as her touch.

'And I know you' I replied. 'You're my writer – aren't you?'

Ode To A Bully

Don't shout at me and scowl and puff
I'm not your wife and I've had enough.
I'm not scared of you, so get control
This red hostility makes you look old.

It might be time to change your ways
And end up happier for your final days
You're spoilt and obviously been allowed
To behave like this, even in a crowd.

Remember, I'm no violet and I'll not shrink
And I really don't like the way you think.
So – take a deep breath and slow your rhythm
I'll wait and assure you of forgiveness given.

Pet Tale

I was brought up with pets as a child
Outside cats both bad-mannered and wild
Sweet tempered retrievers with puppies galore
Danced about on the stone pantry floor.

My sister had a white rat called Blanche
Which would bite you if it got a chance
Came the day it escaped, slinking out of its cage
I was pleased - but my sibling enraged.

Puss-a-titis and Tit-a-pusses the cats
Had a well known addiction to rats
This sugared version was a gourmet meal
All they left was the tail and one heel.

Then such crying and dramas ensued
With the little girl right off her food
Till our father relented and said for the sake
Of some peace and quiet he would get her a snake.

Schism

How do these things begin and how can they end
When each one is certain that the rift will never mend
How can words be said or written to cause such a breach
Between sisters or friends who quickly will impeach
The other to protect themselves against the pain of being
     wrong
And know the loss and sense of guilt will go on and on
     and on.

Witnesses observe and some will doubtless feel some glee
At the spectacle of these 'inseparables' enduring the
     misery
Of schism in its fullest sense, a chasm deep and wide
Which it is unlikely time with healing will provide.
So years will doubtless roll on by and the moment will be
     lost
Before either woman starts to count the full and terrible
     cost.

And will there be at the end of the life-cycle for each one
A rage at the lost times when something might have been
     done
Or instead will the faces of those involved in the rift
Show the signs of embitterment instead of the lift

Of tranquillity earned from a life filled with love
Before meeting their maker in heaven above.

I imagine St Peter will ask at the gate
Why no chances were taken for the storm to abate
From wild condemnation and exaggerated stories
From endless discussion to provide the theories
Of righteousness which didn't really explain
That you only could lose, there was nothing to gain.

Sleeping With Your Husband

Dark urine struck the spotless pan below
The pressure was tremendous, with interrupted flow
I waited for the string of released gas and grunt of
    pleasure
Before the half-hearted attempt to press the flush.

Climbing back in with long contented sigh
He puts his freezing cold soles against my warm thigh.

Well yes, it was hot. The air was almost putrid in the
    stillness
But he threw his bedclothes over me and I fretted with
    my hotness
Then, clearly, he felt chilly and took it all back – causing
    me coldness
Unaware, he continued to snort those unattractive pig
    noises – such stress
When you have to listen to it hour after hour in the
    midsummer darkness
Knowing that light will come early, and though the sun
    brings happiness
How can you manage without enough sleep?

Dwelling on, you try to keep your eyes shut, but really
    it's quite hopeless
Still, you're glad because when his leg flops over, you
    aren't defenceless
And can tense your neatly tucked thighs against the
    impact of a not weightless
Lump of meat that pre-empts the arm, which hovers like
    a great crane, unless
Through some mystic helpline he lets it fall where it
    should at his side, and bless
His heart he doesn't know that sleeping with him can
    make a maiden feel distress
When wakefulness brings a pounding head and no
    discipline not to be cross.

Does this mean that you want to move out?
Do you feel that you can't face another night at his side?
Is it too much just lying waiting for sleep sure that,
    should it come, it won't stay?
Yes, yes and yes, until he wakes himself and puts his arms
    around you, tells you he loves you, then it's 'No'!

The Christmas Present

The parcel seemed heavy and everyone knew that, when unwrapped, the contents would be valuable.

It was Christmas time and the parcel had been lying under the tree for two days. The children had all looked at it carefully, wondering what he'd chosen this time but not daring to touch it, and now their mother started to pull the string and begin the long process of discovery. The suspense, she said, was killing her.

The father did this every year and it was all part of the occasion – his gift to her, especially.

They were in the sitting room of the family home. It was a beautiful big Georgian house and this room was the finest of all. A marbled fireplace surrounded by deep sofas and antique tables, wonderful paintings with discreet lighting furnished the bulk of the room. At one end the Christmas tree had been placed next to the grand piano as usual. The thick velvet curtains had been pulled against the cold and dark outside. It was warm and there was a hint of wood-smoke. It was perfect.

The mother sat on the floor under the tree. The sheen of her black satin trousers reflected the Christmas lights above and she was perfumed and elegant as always. Her husband stood nearby, watching her, holding his usual tipple of pink gin and smiling slightly. He'd always spoiled her – taken pride in buying her something important and spending time wrapping several layers to prolong the process of anticipation.

All six children were there, five daughters and one son plus two obedient dogs waiting by the fire for someone to return and fuss them.

Concentrating on her task, the woman removed the twine and brown paper to reveal what the rest of the family knew would be the first of many layers of decorated wrapping. In between each sheet there would be a little card or a chocolate, just like 'pass the parcel' at a children's party, only there's only one recipient.

She smiled up at her husband - the intimacy of their relationship was never more evident than when he bought her something new, like then.

With each layer of paper revealing the next little treat as well as the care that was taken to prepare it all, she took another sip of her gin and tonic.

She muttered impatiently from time to time but she knew that she had to do this properly. 'Can someone please get me another drink?' she demanded.

The children, had all found a vantage point from which to watch the process. The youngest, and only boy of the family, kept edging nearer to his mother so that he could peer into the wrapping to see what the next treat would be. He was only four and had been allowed to stay up as a special treat for Christmas Eve. His dark brown eyes looked huge in the baby face with its flushed cheeks topped with hair that wouldn't lie down. She had already cautioned him about getting too near – he might spill her drink she'd said.

The sisters were more experienced and kept a distance. The youngest had crawled up onto Claire's lap and put her little arms around her fifteen year old sisters neck. Claire glanced at the eldest, Catherine, to convey pleasure that her lap had been chosen this time, but Catherine wasn't really interested because her boyfriend Bill said he would be coming round later. One of the other two had gone to replenish her mother's glass and the final daughter lay on her tummy towards the back of the tree, twirling a silver bauble with her finger and sticking her tongue out to check her reflection. But then she was only 7.

There seemed to be more layers than usual. The mother's face bent over her task and there was a slight tremor in her fingers. The father stirred and the sisters exchanged uneasy glances.

There was silence. No one dared to speak and the only noises came from the fire crackling. 'Quiet boys' said the man as the dogs had also registered the atmosphere and risen to their feet in expectation.

'Well, this is all very nice,' the mother spoke suddenly. 'I'm sure I must be near the end by now. Claire, go and get me a proper drink this time and make sure I can taste the gin.' She glared at the unfortunate daughter who had previously failed at this task.

Claire put the child down from her lap and rose to fulfil the request. She looked angry - yet again, a superb family evening was about to be ruined by her oldest enemy - alcohol.

In the pantry Claire decided that the best course of action was to pour the contents of the bottle of gin down the sink. As the last drops hit the plug, she put some angostura bitters into the glass of tonic water to help mask the missing spirit. Two cubes of ice and the cocktail was ready.

Back in the sitting room it was clear that the final stage of unwrapping had been reached. The mother reached up, took the glass wordlessly from Claire and put it down on the carpet next to her. She licked her lips in anticipation and tore back the final layer. She opened the box and strained to carefully lift out the tissue wrapped gift. It was a heavy decorative plate about eight inches in diameter, an ugly thing exhibiting porcelain reptiles on moss and grass.

She seemed confused and looked up at her husband. 'Don't you like it Sweetheart?' he sounded sad.

Holding the plate in both hands she gazed at it again. 'Well thank you Darling. I can see that this is a very valuable piece and I'll treasure it.'

Everyone watched silently as she climbed stiffly to her feet. The father helped her and clutching her drink with one hand and the plate with the other she walked over to the fireplace. She took a sip of her drink and instantly her face changed. An expression of loathing contorted her face. She was usually so pretty to look at, but not then.

The children knew the signs and started to leave the room. The oldest ensuring that the youngest were away before the storm broke. The dogs followed.

Her mother caught up with Claire in the hall, who noticed that her mother was holding her plate against her chest.

'How dare you?' she screamed 'When I say I want a drink, I expect to get one and not have my orders defied – especially by you.'

Claire turned away from her but her hair was grabbed and the pressure of her mother's furious grasp forced the young girl down. Within seconds Claire was on the floor, lying on her back, shoulders pinned to the ground by the larger woman. She couldn't protect herself. In the doorway behind her Claire could see her stunned father, but he didn't move to help.

The woman was mad. Holding her Christmas present, the expensive and heavy plate in the air above her head with both hands, she screamed at her daughter, 'I hate you. I've always hated you. You with your secret green eyes. I'm going to kill you.'

Claire closed her eyes and turned her face to try and take the blow on one side - she was too terrified to speak.

There was a rushing noise and a thump. Claire lay still - too shocked to move. Her mother lay on her side at Claire's feet and she was crying. Her husband knelt next to her and held her in his arms. 'There there' he said.

Claire's rescuer lifted her to her feet. 'Hello Bill' she said in a shaky voice and burst into tears. He led the girl away towards the kitchen at the far end of the house where her siblings surrounded her protectively.

Claire mopped up her tears and gradually stopped shaking. She felt the weight of habitual sorrow at her mother's dislike of her and was quiet.

Bill put his arm round Catherine. 'I'm so glad I came round. I was just in the nick of time. Does your mother often behave like this?' He sounded appalled.

'No of course not.' Catherine lied. 'She's just had a bit too much to drink tonight.....' she stuttered to a stop unable to look at anyone.

Bill nodded his acceptance. 'Here Catherine I've bought you a present. I hope you don't mind but we have a family tradition that if you really care about someone then their Christmas present should be wrapped up at least ten different ways and have a little treat in between the layers.'

'Crumbs,' said Catherine looking at Claire, 'Just don't tell me it's a plate with snakes on it.'

So Good For His Eczema

I watched my twin boys play in the rock pool
In that heady summer before starting school
Blond heads bent as they shared the chat
Of what to do here and where to put that.

They were making a hole that would be a great harbour
For small plastic boats – and throughout their labour
The sun shone down on their sandy backs
As they patted and dug and filled in the cracks.

I remembered these days from my own far-off youth
Time filled with sunshine when shielded from truth
Of how hard life could be, how dismal the fact
Of how few you could trust - the real impact.

Imagine then, how protective I'd be
Of my little ones' perfect day by the sea.
When two older women appeared in our view
I had no inkling or instinct at what they might do.

Why should I think of them as a day changer?
Or that my children could end up in danger?
I'd noticed the dog, a small angry terrier
Which pulled and tugged at its leash of leather

One woman leaned down and undid the strap
Releasing the beastie which, with a loud slap,
Flung itself happily into our pool of water
The owner clapped hands and said through her laughter

'Sooooo good for his eczema.'

"Boys! OUT"

Off Chile On A Cruise Ship

Looking across the choppy grey waters near the head of the inlet and waiting for the small deluxe ship to swing around at anchor, as it had all day, I stare again at the tiny bright green building on the opposite shore.

There are two windows only visible so the door must be at the side and in the lea of the prevailing wind. The roof is tin and one tunnelled chimney suggests warmth available – as does the stack of logs, bigger than the shack itself and covered by a modest roof of its own. There are no poles or wires, so no electricity – maybe paraffin lamps or just candles light the interior.

There is an enclosure by the water for chickens and a larger area of fencing with two sheep. There's a polytunnel and some cultivated patches and on the water itself at a small inlet is a boat. It rains most of the year here, so no problems with fresh water and I suppose the sewage is tossed on the land or into the sea.

This is self-sufficiency since there's no road – no access other than by foot over rough terrain or boat to the modest port several miles away.

And what, I wonder, must the inhabitants of this property think as they see this big white presence in their view. Maybe an element of wonder, of envy – but if they knew more would they ultimately want to change places with some of the over-pampered and indulged people – of both genders – on this lovely ship. I hope not. What they have there seems almost perfect to me.

Platitudinous Claptrap

I woke for the weather forecast early that day
It was of great importance because what she might say
Would affect what I wore for that first interview
For the job that I felt was my perfect due.

I had hung several outfits on the back of the door
And 'accessorised' each to meet latest fashion lore
But, if it rained or was foggy or terribly cold
I'd have to change everything. I did need to be told.

Right then - there she is smiling on my television screen
And I thought she looked fat today, but happy and serene
She'd never know that I watched her with a curling sneer
But she repaid me anyway when the weather news came
    clear.

'The day is starting cloudy but there's trouble coming
    through
with a chance of rain and thunder and strong winds
    possibly due
We could expect some hail and perhaps some sleet and
    snow
I've had a good look at the charts but I don't really know.

On the other hand it could be warm. You can never rule
    it out
And I'm sure I saw a patch of blue over Spain or
    thereabouts
And it could spread north as the day goes on. But just in
    case I'm wrong
Make sure you take a warm coat, hat, scarf, gloves and
    boots along.'

She signed off with her usual 'Have a really lovely day…'
 Feeling furious, I'd heard enough – no more nonsense –
    no way
I switched off her smug unpleasant face with a satisfying
    snap
I'd heard enough today of her platitudinous claptrap!

Searching For Simon

Difficult Recurring Dream

I can smell the river, the mud and debris swirling near
    the shore and
I can hear the water slapping hard against the pier.
I can feel the drizzle falling softly on the dirty alley
    leading to the edge and
beneath my hand my heartbeat fast with fear.

In the darkness I can touch cold metal on the ancient
    door and
I move slowly forward to the bottom of the stair.
I know my pain and anguish which, in order to assuage
    them,
have conquered me and forced me to be there.

Where is my son, my final child? Who, now so tall, is in
    my dream
once more a little one with thick blond hair.
I climb and search along the endless corridors but hope
    to make no noise.
I dare not; there is danger everywhere.

Time passes, the pressure on me mounts and the foreign
    hostile atmosphere pervades the cold stale air.
At last I reach the reckoning room. It's empty and there's
    no escape.
But who, I wonder, will find me and subsequently care?

The window can be opened and, once done, I feel the
    breeze
Of marshland grass and wetness layer
itself across my face and over my outstretched arms,
reaching out in supplication and pessimistic prayer.

I can see a light approaching. I watch, since nothing else
    is moving, and
wiping my tears into the night I peer
Exaggerated by hope, I think that I see him, I hear him
    and I know him.
It is him, my darling boy, my final child, my dear.

The Speaker's Wife

I heard him immediately as I walked across the crowded dining room, navigating tables and chairs against the rhythmical rise and fall of the ship.

'It's a disgrace' he bellowed. 'I have been with this shipping line many times and I have never heard anything so appalling'.

The object of this ranting, a Phillipino waiter, was arranging plates crouched before his serving trolley, apparently ignoring the tirade. But there was no impertinence in his manner, just embarrassment.

The shouter – an overweight, bearded man wearing cut off trousers and a cheap striped tee shirt, suddenly looked up and saw me standing by my usual chair. Like everyone else in the vicinity I was watching him. He strode angrily towards me, knocking into the back of another passenger's chair on the way.

'What are you staring at?' he demanded, spittle spraying his beard.

'I'm looking at you making an exhibition of yourself' I spoke quietly.

'Well, I don't know who you think you are' he was shouting again, 'You're only the speaker's wife'. He took another step nearer whilst I held my ground but noticed two waiters approaching from the side. 'I bet you haven't even paid to come on this ship' he roared.

In a low calm voice I deliberately smiled up at him.

'Whatever makes you think that? Why would I not pay to come and spend time with someone like you?'

Wheelchair

I've hurt myself and can't believe that such a simple
    tumble
Would cause such fuss, so much pain and huge desire to
    grumble
The foot is black and swollen, with skin stretched taut
    and thin
So – ice pack on, limb held high, smile fixed rigid, I'm
    now strapped in
 To this horrible bloody wheelchair.

And suddenly everyone sees me but nobody thinks I can
    hear
'How is she today?' they ask kindly over my head and
    into the air
to my husband who minds that I'm injured but secretly
    loves all the stir
and attention from people who, up until then, hadn't
    noticed we were there
 And I'm deaf in this brute of a wheelchair.

'It looks very nasty' I must say, the legions repeat one by
    one
'Does it keep her awake? Such a shame. She must mind
    missing all the fun'

My beloved answers all questions sweetly, whilst
    uselessly adjusting my shawl
Then with flick of his wrist, he whizzes me round so that
    now I am facing the wall.
 And I'm blind in this bastard wheelchair.

The doctor wanted to see me. He asked: Is she getting
    along?
With pain control and some mobility – important not to
    go wrong
With the drugs, the strapping and physio. Discussion
    between them was earnest
'Oh she's doing so well' said my lover. Said the doctor
    'she still has to rest'.
 And I'm mute in the damned wheelchair.

I continued seething inwards, getting better was
    laboriously slow
And my darling stopped asking solicitously. My zone had
    become 'no go!'
Self-centredness ruled until my interest was diverted - I
    spotted a rival chair
There sat a woman so clearly in pain, with angelic smile
    and snowy white hair.

She watched me serenely as I approached and her smile
    became a grin
'Are you better today?' she asked sweetly but I was hit
    with chagrin
and felt awful for all those black moments when I had
    felt angry and blue
so ashamed of myself for complaining at all when faced
    with suffering true.

'I'm fine' I said quickly and felt it, my concern now
    transferred to this other
whose form attested to attack by disease which her thin
    blanket couldn't cover.
Though I knew her not at all, her courage and acceptance
    were plain
for this wonderful person would not get well and she'd
    never walk again

She would spend all her days in her motorised, highly
    sophisticated
State-of-the-art, life-enhancing and wonderful
    wheelchair.

Oh Mr Puccini

Oh Mr Puccini how you have changed my life
With the wonderful works that defined your own
Even though Verdi led the way with his dramatic art
including 'Nabucco' fifteen years before you were born.

With your love for 'verismo' you wrote 'La Boheme'
An opera I adore, and which allows me to weep
Unrestrainedly coaxed by your music. The sadness and
    the beauty
Of young love, threatened then extinguished by disease
    and death.

'Madam Butterfly' - such loyalty, hopefulness, desertion
    and despair.
 'Tosca' with its tale of feminine honour and political
    corruption.
These, and others, your typically Italian gift for delightful
    melody -
A medium for dramatic expression – adored by your
    public both then and now.

But Oh Mr Puccini, I especially love your legacy, here in
    the 21st century

Where there is little 'romanticism' just poor manners,
    obesity and tattoos.
So, I put you on in my kitchen or car and am taken away
    by the loveliness
Of those voices, that music, the memories of perfect
    theatre. Thank you.

Pretentiousness

I've just come in to a nice pile of money
So the financial future looks wonderfully sunny
My husband's delighted and I feel serene
The first thing I'll get is someone in to clean.

Now where shall we live and what about schools
We can buy a big mansion with parkland and pools
I quite fancy Surrey or Berkshire perhaps
With deep marbled bathtubs and gold-plated taps.

We may want a little white house by the sea
For all of the leisure time now that we're free
Of worry and stresses that can't take their toll
I think we should look on the Costa del Sol.

My fingers and toes will be well manicured
My personal trainer, young, fit and assured
Of success with my fitness and collagen troubles
After weights, bikes and saunas and Jacuzzi bubbles

My hair won't be mousy but sleek and highlighted
My make-up expensive, my skin clear, unblighted
By lesions and spots caused by cheap creams and sticks
The first place I'll go to should be Harvey Nicks!

I have a long list and I think I will buy
Clothes, bags, shoes, accessories, new perfumes I'll try
I'll wander the aisles feeling calm affectation
Pretending I'm used to all this ostentation

With rings on my fingers and jewellery galore
I wonder, once started, if I'll only want more
Of the fabulous items that money can buy
I'm just so excited, I'm really quite high.

But, I know me, I know me, I know my own soul
Why should I exceed on my first stated goal
Of husband and children and friends I adore
With a home and a garden, why should I have more?

I've enjoyed all the thinking of life grandiose
Of prancing around with an elevated nose
But the truth is I know of children elsewhere
Living in squalor with no one to care.

So, we'll have a good think my hubby and me
I'm sure he'll support me and that we'll agree
On what is the best place to share this new wealth
Giving shelter and kindness, protection and health.

Pretentiousness, arrogance, grandiloquence
Are not things that suit me and I have a sense
Of relief that I can carry on being me
Just an ordinary woman, I'm content and happy.

The Dinner Party

The table's all set and the menu complete
It's taken all day and I'm dead on my feet
The house is now tidy it's all nice and clean
There's far too much wine but I hate being mean.

We both have a shower and I put on my face
And I pick up his clothes left all over the place
He smiles at me sweetly and tells me he loves me
So I kiss him, ignoring my tiredness completely.

And here they all are, six really nice friends
Clearly glad to be with us, and everyone tends
To speak at the same time for the first little while
Till we give them a drink with a word or a smile.

We're all sitting down and the soup looks delicious
I've forgotten the morning and chopping knife vicious
Oh dear, what's the matter, it was only a tap
But Jo's dropped her gazpachio all over her lap.

Once mopped up she gives us a tremulous grin
And I wonder if she just had far too much gin
The next thing she has is a string of loud hiccoughs
We're careful – she's a dodgy psychological make-up.

My food was delicious and worth the hard work
I've never been lazy and I'll never shirk
From making an effort, but think it's a pity
Such triumphs don't last into per-pet-uity.

I'd decided on steaks and so asked everyone
How much or how little they like them to be done
Peter cut into his with gusto and vigour
Then pushed it away – 'This one's still got rigor!'

His wife is my mate, I can see that she's cross
'Pass your plate over' she ordered. He knows whose boss.
His smile was quite sickly, but he ate all the meat
She'd passed over to him and he said 'You're so sweet.'

Hot cheese was perfect, the puddings were fab
The coffee steamed gently, there were chocolates to grab
We all felt so comfy, so full and content
Conversation was easy, no sign of dissent.

So, who would choose evenings to argue and bicker
When alternatives equal good food and fine liquor.
With people you like who say 'You're just the best
At providing so well – the perfect hostess.

The Spider

I am the spider on the beam
That caught and ate the fly on the wall
So now I can see, hear and understand
What they are saying and what they each mean.

'You're so boring these days and your ideas are dated
And you lack curiosity' the man took a gulp of his whisky
    and waited.
She reacted at once then regretted it showed as trembling
    and flushing she rose
From her chair - smoothed out her sweater and tidied
    her hair.
Collecting herself for the words she would say, shoulders
    back – stand tall
As her father would tell her. Nice low voice, calm now.
    Don't feel small
She said 'What lies over the horizon, inside the box and
    behind the door,
Holds no interest for me. Not any more.
You've taken my world and ripped it apart.
I feel empty and lonely. You've broken my heart.
'You're pathetic' he snarled, sipped again and glared
    angrily over the rim.

From my view at the top, as I witnessed this scene – I
    hurt for her and hated him.
'I'm so far ahead of you…' she started to say but he
    silenced her as, leaning
red-faced and hostile, he passed wind, a gesture so rude,
    so basic – demeaning.
From my roost high above, I observed her chest heave
As, turning away with a shrug, she prepared to leave.

'What is it that makes you think you know more than
    me?'
Keen to torment her he said 'Come on then – Let's see'
His face, once so handsome, was lined now and creased
With his vituperative lifestyle. His ignorance of peace.
She turned squarely towards him and gave a small smile
'There's part of me, precious and rare, you can't access
    now -You haven't for a while
As she lifted her eyes did she see me, she started to sway
"I can see beauty in every small thing, in each scent and
    taste from my first waking moment to the end of my
    day.
And it no longer matters that you can't see
All those wonders spread out to enjoy
Those simple experiences, love, wonder and joy
I feel immensely sorry for you.'

If I'm ever asked just what happened that day
I would take the opportunity and have my say.
I'd tell how he'd punched her and hit her hard on her
    face,
That this man was a bully, an ogre, a disgrace.
I 'd reveal how she wept as he sat down in his chair
And lifted his paper as if she wasn't there

How she'd picked up his ashtray and with eyes dark as
    lead,
she gone round behind him and struck hard on his head
I would tell them that I had to jump back on my beam
as his blood spurted out in a volcanic stream
And how kneeling before him with a knife from her coat
I had watched as she carefully cut her own throat.

I would have told them if they'd asked what I'd seen
But… I am only the spider on the beam
That caught and ate the fly on the wall
And that now I can see, hear and understand
What they are saying and what they each mean.

But nobody asked me.

Sandra The Train Passenger

There was quite a crowd on the 4.22pm from Euston to Northampton. One of the last to arrive, and clearly fortunate to get a seat, was Sandra.

Sandra pushed her way into the window seat opposite me, past the earnest businesswoman with her laptop on her lap. "Scuse me; let me by; 'scuse me' she bellowed. The businesswoman smiled politely and tried to refocus on her work once her neighbour had settled herself, bag in the rack above, handbag on lap.

Sandra stood suddenly 'Oh there you are Sue' she hollered at a tiny birdlike women across the aisle. 'Where's Bev?' she roared. 'Has anyone seen Bev? Oh, it's alright, she's over there. You alright Bev? Got a good seat?' Everyone in the carriage was looking at her now.

Nodding vigorously obviously satisfied that all was well, she sat down abruptly. Then a noisy dialogue started across the woman next to her, across the aisle, over the man at her side to Sue.

'Great day weren't it?' Sandra asked

Sue nodded back at her, looking embarrassed. The rest of us knew that we were included in the dialogue now and waited to hear about their day. The man next to me as well as the one opposite Sue both pulled their newspapers higher and gave them a little shake. Clear signs that they did not want to be bothered.

Businesswoman gave a tired smile at the man next to Sue. He rose immediately and spoke to Sandra 'Would you like to sit next to your friend?'

Without a word Sandra rose again and collecting her bags she said "Scuse me, let me by, 'Scuse me' at the harassed woman in her way.

'I'm over 'ere now Bev.' Sandra roared down the train to her other friend. The train had started and was going at speed so she sat down quickly. The two women then began a noisy and giggly conversation about someone they both knew who 'often went outside without her knickers on'. The men with the raised newspapers gave them another shake.

The man opposite me played with his mobile 'phone then leaving it on the table in front of him, he dozed off; the businesswoman became engrossed once more in her laptop and I rested my head on the window and gazed at the countryside speeding by.

Suddenly the mobile 'phone on the table started its tune. The man slept.

Sandra obviously couldn't bear it. The idea of someone not answering a call was incomprehensible.

"Scuse me. Oy you over there asleep. 'Scuse me' she shouted. 'Answer yer 'phone. Yer 'phones ringing Mate'. But he slept without stirring.

A new focus for discussion between Sandra and Sue, and not to forget Bev. 'Oy Bev. Do yer know what? There's a fella here who's not answered his 'phone. It's been ringing ages.'

Sandra stared at the man and then nudged Sue hard in the ribs. 'Ere Sue do you suppose he's dead?' She rose to her feet to reach past the businesswoman. I imagined she wanted to give him a shake or something but at that moment the sleeping unfortunate opened his mouth and let out a huge snore'.

The Charity Fair

Well, here we all are in the old Village Hall
The resident worthies have set up their stalls
The trestles are groaning with home produced fare
And even Her Ladyship has agreed to be there.

There's a babble of chatter, some laughter and cups
Being rattled in the kitchen before they're filled up
With nearly off milk and undrinkable tea
For which we're all happy to pay 25p.

There's a greeting of old friends, a whoop of delight
When an old fox fur collar held up in the light
Proved too much for Molly to try and resist
Now she's trying to think what to take off her list.

The bookstall as usual is a tremendous success
£1 for a first edition, the seller would take less
She's so happy to be there, so glad to be asked
And feels useful, important and good at her task.

The china stall's causing a lot of attention
Some lovely but mostly too ghastly to mention
An old Toby jug does the rounds every year
I almost look forward to seeing him here.

Some children are there and behaving quite well
'Cos they're picking their way through the items on sale
On the table set aside for games, puzzles and toys
As usual the girls get pushed aside by the boys.

In wafts the woman who thinks she's the tops
The endlessly difficult and spiteful Mrs Potts
She gazes around her to see whom she might know
Unaware that the sight of her makes some decide to go.

With a supercilious air, nose and eyebrows aloft
She picks over Annie's fresh bread to see if it's soft
The vicar moves over, he can see Annie's distress
But he must protect Mrs P - she's his benefactress.

'Vicar – hello.' she roars in a voice heavy with inflection
So that everyone there knows of her godly connection
Her heavy lined face, lots of colour and moustache
Are obliterated by her mouth, a deep purple gash.

At the bric-a-brac stall two fat ladies collide
Pick up things that have dropped and move to the side
To recover their dignity, calmness and poise
Hardly anyone's noticed because of the noise.

The vicar is now on the stage looking fearfully
Down at his brood, he looks out of place and silly
He'd agreed to a face-paint, for charity you see
And they've gone the whole hog and designed a monkey.

He says 'Well, thank you all so much for coming here
today
The committee are delighted and they've just asked me
to say
That the money raised, over £500, is going to the poor

And could some of you stay to help clear up?' There's an
    unseemly rush to the door.

I love these local events – they're good for the
    community
For young and old villagers and especially the elderly
It's the heart of the week for most of them there
A chance to be English to communicate and share.

Ode To Really Old Women

There was once an old lady with hair snowy white
Who said 'fuck it' and laughingly called me a 'shite'
I couldn't believe that this elegant crone
Felt no need for remorse - she'd no crime to atone.

This experience caused me a change in perception
And I looked afresh at her generation.
I saw the meaninglessness of so many words -
Useless, irrelevant and completely absurd.

The time comes when one should no longer worry
And can leave all the fussing about in a hurry
To the next lot down – the middle-aged girls
Not yet ready to receive ancient pearls.

It's the situation when you no longer care
About things you can't change – poof, gone into the air
And there's confidence then for the final stages
with no place for upsets, tantrums and rages.

Instead there's serenity for facing what's next
No point in denying death, no need to be vexed
With what you can't change but there's that requirement
To keep dignity going through and after retirement.

So when my time comes please make sure that I
Can lie with my face turned full to the sky
With lace at my throat and a rose on my linen
The soft touch of velvet and the kiss of my children.

Mini Sagas

The Princess in the Tower

Fragrancia let down her hair. A tiny prince climbed up and made love to her. Exhausted, he lay sleeping. With his sword she cut her plaits and tied them to his belt. She absailed down. Her hefty weight snapped his fragile back. Who could love her now, fragrance notwithstanding?

To Wilfred and Edith a Happy Event

Lonely when they retired, they met at a writers group and became lovers. Wilfred was 65 and a widower and Edie a widow of 61. He wanted a second career but she sought penance for past crimes – murder when nursing the vulnerable sick. "He doesn't look well," thought Edie.

Targets

Every night he pretended to shoot himself in front of her. He worried that this scene in his play spoilt the performance. "Hold the gun higher" she suggested. "Why not put it in your mouth?" She rose and stood

before him. "Go on my Darling, pull the trigger".
BANG.

Ending

They had a troubled marriage. She couldn't swim and avoided water but agreed to a cruise "Get to know each other again," he'd said. "This is perfect – stand on the rail" he whispered sexily in her ear. "Goodbye Darling" He called cheerily as he pushed her over the side.

Donation

He earned well for his twenty sperm donations whilst at university. The nurse admired him – "Good genes" she thought. At the last session he asked her if she had any children. "Oh yes" she smiled and showed him a photograph of a toddler in his own image. Oh No!